Mimar Houses

MIMAR HOUSES

A MIMAR COLLECTION

Concept Media

MIMAR HOUSES is a collection of articles
originally featured in MIMAR© issue numbers 1,
2, 3, 4, 5, 6, 9, 12, 13, 15, 19 and 22.

Published by Concept Media Pte Ltd
1 Grange Road, 05-11/12 Orchard Building
Singapore 0923

First Edition: October 1987

ISBN: 9971-84-867-8

Production: Patricia Theseira
Design: Viscom Design Associates

Typesetting: Eurasia Press
Colour separations: Sixty-Six Lithographic Pte
    Ltd, Scantrans Pte Ltd and Eurasia Press.
Printed and bound in Singapore by Eurasia Press.

Cover: Al Sulaiman Palace, Jeddah. Photograph
    courtesy of A.W. El-Wakil.
Frontispiece: Benjelloun House, Marrakesh.
    Photograph: Jacques Bétant.

CONTENTS

Introduction

PART ONE

Individual Houses

PART TWO

House Types

Introduction

The individual family residence is a complex phenomenon just as it is a faithful reflection — to the degree that the inhabitants had a part in shaping it — of the needs, tastes, and aspirations of the client. If one is not the original owner of a newly-acquired abode, among the first things one does is to adapt the interior spaces to one's own requirements. Whereas if the future inhabitants of a domestic environment participated as clients in the initial conception and design (along with an architect or builder), the result invariably involves the satisfaction of multiple personal desires — expressed privately or publicly, internally or externally.

To enter a domestic interior is to advance into the intimate life of individuals and families. Degrees of privacy are provided for in any residential space, East or West, but in dwellings of the Orient spaces tend to be organised in a more rigidly hierarchical fashion. Often clear distinctions are made between reception areas for strangers or family acquaintances and those areas for family group activities where males and females mingle freely. This is frequently less characteristic of Western homes, where life-styles can be more informal. Notions of privacy are of course based upon social structure and social mores, upon functional uses, but also upon codes or conventions of what is *presentable,* that is to say, objects, images or even sounds that reflect the inner personal sentiments, memories, devotions of the individuals who inhabit. The houses published in this volume, be they contemporary or historical, illustrate the tremendous latitude that exists in degrees and nature of privacy, from that of an Arabian sheik to that of the Central Asian nomads' tent.

A number of the examples have a common trait, namely the organisation of living spaces around a central space — often open to the sky. This "room without a roof", situated as it is at the heart of the plan, functions as a distribution space for the adjacent rooms, whether it is the Gülgönen or Tiptus houses, or the underground houses of China. While climate and life-styles (both rural and urban) make the courtyard a convenient, recurring element, it also can be given a symbolic interpretation as the heart of home in many cultures, particularly as the dwelling in Africa, the Middle East and parts of Asia is *introverted* and focused on this court. Hence, with little or no exterior decoration to demarcate one house from another on the typical North African street, the walls of courts can also become surfaces where decoration is lavished.

Moreover, in houses where a central court is not a feature, outdoor spaces in the form of a garden become an extension of, or are incorporated into the indoor living spaces. A Moroccan *riad* is a landscaped room without a roof, on the scale of Mr. Benjelloun's garden, with fountains and pools. Or, the garden at Geoffrey Bawa's country residence is almost sculpted out of the wild lush foliage and furnished with objects that range from the fanciful to the fantastic: statues, pots, masks ...

Hierarchies of spaces for intimate private use, semi-private reception, or for open display (of wealth, fantasy) can also be linked to choices in decoration. Muslim dwellings in many parts of the world have traditionally made a clear distinction between the public facade presented on the street, characteristically lacking in ostentatious ornamentation, and rich embellishment of the interiors. The Marrakesh week-end house of Mr. Benjelloun or Fida Ali's 17the Street house, each in their own way, maintain this distinction, whereas the majority of the contemporary examples from Kuwait published here do not do so at all. The unrestrained exhibitionism of the Western-inspired, free-standing villa whose applied decoration is derived neither from the structural system nor from traditional vocabularies or motifs: the decor is a confused mixture of materials, colors and forms reflecting a confused sense of identity and cultural values. Clearly, the problem is *not* that the wealth of decoration is expressed on the exterior rather than the interior — stucco work in Yemen or carved woodwork of Jeddah's old house are beautiful examples of exterior ornamentation; it is that there is no stylistic consistency, no rationale beyond a desire to show off, to draw attention to oneself.

The significance of certain houses in this volume, combining traditional features with modern needs and tastes, resides in the architect and/or client opting to depart from rigorous conservative conventions (for instance, set patterns or color combinations for Moroccan mosaic-work) and to innovate. This has invariably involved a production process where traditional craftsmen are employed at an early stage of conception and execution — not after the house is already up. While it is true that such experiments are often only affordable by a rich elite, the results can prove to be instructive models for future collaboration between modern professionals and indigenous craftsmen.

Highly debatable consequences can occur when the political authorities of a society decree that a particular *style* of architecture is to be preferred throughout the land. This is the case in present day Morocco, where King Hasan II has publicly urged adoption of traditional materials and decorative forms for all new constructions. While this is one extreme case of trying to legislate questions of taste, more subtle actions are possible, as in the case of Mr. Cakirhan in Turkey, who was asked to advise on all future restorations in his region, or in the case of the Tiptus House, the Society of Architects in Thailand gave it one of its prestigious awards. At issue is the matter of *patronage,* not so much of public institutional buildings but of private residential architecture. When the individual client has the financial means to achieve the dwelling of his dreams, free societies can only respect personal tastes. Legislation can take the form, as it has in some Western societies, of guidelines or codes intended to protect the natural qualities of a site or the existing built *milieu* if it is of historical interest.

Ultimately, the quality in contemporary house design in the developing world will depend upon the client, his sensitivity to his own cultural heritage and an open frame of mind towards the eventual use of local, traditional materials and know-how to resolve his needs; and it will depend upon the client's dialogue with the architect, sculptor, designer of his choice. The burden is really preponderantly on the side of the client, for it is his own self-image that is to be given physical shape. If he simply calls upon a draughtsman working in someone else's office to provide him with stereotyped plans for a building permit — which is what occurs in 9 out of 10 cases in Third World countries — then he not only avoids paying an architect's fees but also misses the creative dialogue with an imaginative, informed professional. The complexities arise when a client accepts to give up the easy solution of stereotyped or imitative designs and enters into a viable search for self-expression through his projected dwelling. Many of the excellent houses published in this MIMAR edition would not have become what they are had not the client reflected deeply upon his *own,* instead of imported, cultural values and subsequently attempted to incorporate these in his future abode. The degree and manner by which this was done, with the aid and counsel of professionals has yielded these remarkable examples.

Brian Brace Taylor

Individual Houses

William Willis

Benjelloun House, Marrakesh

Project Data

Location: Marrakesh, adjacent to gardens designed by the French painter Jacques Majorelle when he built his own house there in the 1930's.

Client: Omar Benjelloun, industralist in Casablanca.

Designer: Mr. Bill Willis conceived both the plans of the house and the interior decoration of the spaces.

Completion: March 1983.

Construction: Traditional stone masonry structure, with an exterior coating of tadelakt, which has a lime base and is applied smoothly over a surface and polished to a brilliant finish — traditionally employed in the interiors of hammams.

This striking contemporary interior from Morocco was conceived by a designer from a western background who lives permanently in Marrakesh. Mr Bill Willis offers his clients a remarkable, and occasionally provocative, decorative approach which combines traditional materials, techniques, and geometric motifs with a modernist sensibility. To achieve results such as those present in the Benjelloun house, Mr Willis works in a traditional manner with the Moroccan *maalem* (mimar) craftsman who executes the tilework (*zellige*), woodwork, plasterwork, etc.: for example, most of his intentions are expressed orally rather than with written documents or graphic representations. A *maalem* who is to do the *zellige* covering a chimney, or a wall visits Mr Willis' Atelier, where he is asked to produce samples with a

A zellige is a precut piece of enamelled terracotta tile. A series of standard shapes are used in varying compositions.

given motif and given colour scheme and discusses the possibilities with regard to the surface to be decorated. Few conception drawings are actually employed. The rest is decided on the site. Much of the refinement, or the more spectacular gestures, found in the interior decoration by Mr Willis comes from his knowledge of the materials available, the constraints and freedoms inherent in the techniques, and the fact that he is an outsider to the tradition. He brings his personal, and cultural, sensibility to bear in the creative collaboration.

The house itself is not to be considered a typical Arab dwelling: neither the total plan nor the plan of individual interior spaces reflect an inspiration from traditional Moroccan houses. It is the overall decora-

Below: Main entrance hall. This room, with stairs to upper floor at the far end, communicates with the living-room and a covered gallery facing the garden. Right: The stairs seen from above. The enamelled terracotta tiles used here are called bejmats, *measuring 5 cm x 5 cm, and are traditionally placed on floors whereas the zelliges, or pre-cut tiles are for wall surfaces.*

Text and photographs by Serge Santelli.

tive technique of covering whole surfaces that is typical. *Zelliges* and marble are used together on the floors, and *zelliges* alone on the chimneys and elsewhere. However, the walls are finished with the *tadelakt* technique (mixture of sand, clay and lime projected onto a wall, then covered with a soap and egg-yoke substance and polished with a smooth stone). While the chimneys in the main living rooms are striking visually and sculpturally, they appear to be something of an anachornism in a desert oasis climate. This points up a significant perception about the design work: it is rarely a single, particular element that is beautiful in and of itself, but rather it is the ensemble, the total composition that is spectacular.

One enters the house by a large hall with stairs at the far end of the rectangular space. Immediately to the left is a small bathroom decorated in tones of blue and red, while to the right of the entry hall, perpendicular to it, is the rectangular space of the living room, and divided into two parts by an arcade with columns. On axis, with the arrival in the living room(s) is the main chimney, the upper portion of which

Above: View into the principal living room from entrance hall doorway. A combination of marble and enamelled terracotta tiles are used for the floor. The principal chimney is at the far end of the space.
Right: Intricate patterns formed by traditional Moroccan craftsmen on the surface of the chimney are a major feature of the house.

takes the form of a *mihrab* (seen from the exterior, and apparently of Turkish inspiration), completely covered with geometric motifs made of *zelliges*. A carpet-like mosaic on the wall creates a backdrop to the main chimney. Each of the two living rooms is covered by a cupola. The predominant tones of colour in the living rooms are pink and brown. For example, the joints between the interior facettes of the cupola are high-lighted with brown and black *zelliges* (note: the exterior of these cupolas are pink with *zelliges* of green blue and brown for the joints).

Beyond the living room is located the master bedroom and its bath, also covered by a cupola, an extraordinary hallway, the walls of which are covered with mirrors, links the bedroom, dressing room and bath.

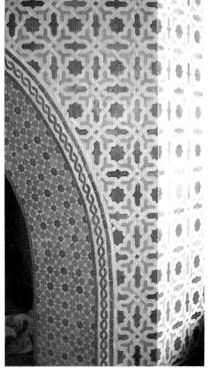

Above: The main living room is divided in two by three arches and columns of white marble. Pink and brown tones prevail in these spaces, from the polished surfaces of the walls executed with the technique known as tadelakt *to* zellige *tile work of the chimneys.*
Left: View of doorways, mirrored walls and cupolas of the hall connecting the master bedroom and the bath.

The colour blue predominates in the decor of the bathroom: dark blue mosaic on the colonnettes, light blue for the walls, which are finished with the *tadelakt* technique.

Stairs in the main entry lead to the first-floor study and bedrooms. Different geometric patterns are used for the risers of these stairs than for the horizontal steps, although the *zelliges* are essentially from the same colour range.

The Benjelloun house, in its traditional ornamentation, is typical of one contemporary trend (and at present a very strong one) in Moroccan architecture to encourage a return to past indigenous values. An assuredly positive result of this demand is to guarantee that traditional craftsmen have work and that the practical knowledge of these crafts is not dying out.

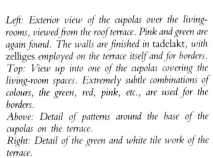

Left: Exterior view of the cupolas over the living-rooms, viewed from the roof terrace. Pink and green are again found. The walls are finished in tadelakt, with zelliges employed on the terrace itself and for borders.
Top: View up into one of the cupolas covering the living-room spaces. Extremely subtle combinations of colours, the green, red, pink, etc., are used for the borders.
Above: Detail of patterns around the base of the cupolas on the terrace.
Right: Detail of the green and white tile work of the terrace.

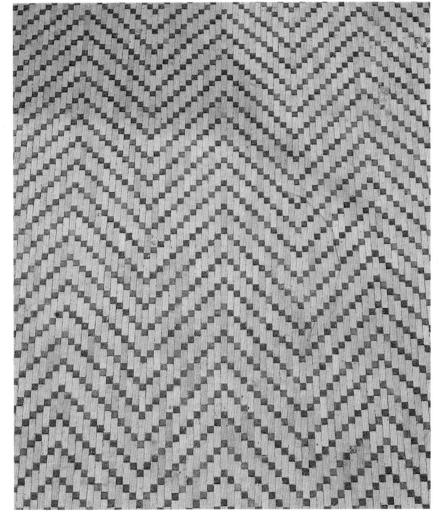

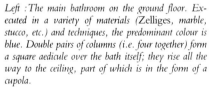

Left : The main bathroom on the ground floor. Executed in a variety of materials (Zelliges, marble,
stucco, etc.) and techniques, the predominant colour is
blue. Double pairs of columns (i.e. four together) form
a square aedicule over the bath itself; they rise all the
way to the ceiling, part of which is in the form of a
cupola.

Top: Cupola and lamp over the main bath. Four
grouped columns are mosaic-covered.

Above: Detail of the decorative pattern found at the
base of the columns, covered with mosaic-work.

Right: Grouped columns frame the mirror in front of
two wash basins. The bath is reflected in the mirror.

Far left: Blue and red decorative motifs characterise a small toilet and wash basin located just off of the main entrance hall in the house. A portion of the cupola is visible, as well as the lamp reflected in the mirror.

Left: Copy of a traditional Moroccan fountain was built in the garden of the house. Note the contrast of the colours used in the fountain, particularly the yellows and blacks, with the softer, quieter colours found inside the house.

Left, below: A second, smaller fountain in the garden.

Mr Benjelloun comes from a well-known and highly influential Moroccan family. An industrialist and proprietor of the Volvo Automotive Franchise for Morocco, Mr Benjelloun is noted for his refined taste in the arts. The house in Marrakesh, which is a second residence for the cool winter months in the North of the country, is situated on a remarkable site near the centre of the city rather than isolated in the suburbs of the oasis.

Mr Serge Santelli, architect and professor at the Ecole des Beaux Arts, is Mimar's correspondent in Paris and North Africa, where he goes frequently for research, teaching and business.

19

Charles Boccara

Abtan House, Marrakesh

Project Data

Client: Mr. Abtan.
Architect: Charles Boccara assisted by Anne Borger.
Completion date: 1984.
Total area (built): 810 square metres.
Contractor: Enterprise Natba.
Materials: Stone, brick, enamelled terracotta, cedarwood.

Located in two hectares of land in the vast residential palm grove outside Marrakesh, the Abtan house is composed spatially into three distinct entities typical of a traditional patio house: (A) private rooms for family life organised around a planted patio; (B) reception area, with a traditional patio which is covered here to become a central salon or *oust ed dar,* and gives access to the dining room and Moroccan sitting room; the Moroccan salon opens onto a (C) labyrinthian garden-house, entirely open to the sky created entirely of vegetation and wood.

These distinct units offer views of typical Moroccan *riads,* a mosaic of orange, olive and palm trees, etc. some perspectives more private, intimate than others.

While the principal structural material is stone (quite common and relatively economical in this region), hand-made bricks are frequently used. Finishings include *tadelakt, zelliges* (mosaic) and cedar for most woodwork.

Below: View of courtyard with fountain and glazed tile paving in the residential part of the house.
Right: Reception wing of the Abtan house as seen from the garden site, with pool in the foreground.

Text by Brian Brace Taylor. Photographs by Christian Lignon. Drawings courtesy of the architect.

Left: View of reception hall from above. Elaborate zellige – work decoration on the floor, and a Moroccan lamp hangs from a cedar wood ceiling.
Above: Main entrance to the house.
Photographs: B.B. Taylor.

Site plan

1. Entrance
2. Gallery
3. Riad
4. Loggia
5. Kiosk for musicians
6. Hall
7. Main salon (oust ed dar)
8. Dining room
9. Moroccan salon with doukhana
10. Bedroom
11. Kitchen and service
12. Pantry
13. Office
14. Guardian's house
15. Atelier

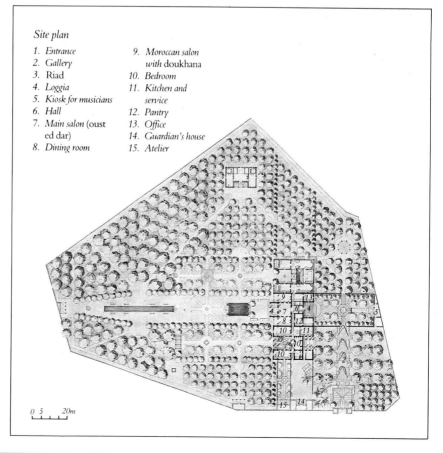

0 5   20m

Left: Entrance hall looking towards the entrance door which is patterned using adapted traditional motifs.
Left, below: Wood ceiling.

Charles Boccara is a French trained architect permanently living and working in Morocco.

Elie Mouyal

Foissac House, Marrakesh

Project Data

Architect: Elie Mouyal.
Client: Mme J. Foissac.
Date: 1984-85.

Among the most recent experiments is this house in the Palmeraie, just outside Marrakesh, for a well-to-do French resident. Interestingly, this was not her first house of earth construction: another was designed and built for her some years ago in the same neighbourhood but by someone else. Having seen other structures by Elie Mouyal built over last two years as part of practical and aesthetic research towards finishing an architectural degree, the client first commissioned construction of a gatehouse in which she now lives — on a new site with principal residence to be located nearby. The gatehouse, which contains a living room with library, bedroom with bath, and kitchen all arranged around a central courtyard (open to the garden on the fourth side), also has a guestroom situated above the entrance passageway to the property.

The simplicity of the plan for the gatehouse does not convey the variety and richness of effect obtained in covering the different volumes: cupola and barrel vaults employing several techniques. Not only do the spaces themselves each have their own physical character (some have surface rendering, others do not), but the quality of light also varies according to type and size of openings through walls that are 50 centimetres thick.

Multiple sources have influenced the conception, the stylistic references, and technical experiments exemplified in this and other recent constructions by Mr. Mouyal. Apart from the excitement elicited by the experiences described by Hassan Fathy in Egypt, there are traces of his appreciation of Hispano-mauresque architecture in Spain and of traditional earth architecture in Morocco itself. He considers his research as operative on two levels, that of evolving an aesthetic vocabulary for contemporary building and, that of evolving the techniques and manpower capable of making earth construction a viable alternative for construction in arid southern Morocco.

Success has been predicated upon several factors, not the least of which has been a client willing to accept a certain measure of experimentation. Also, the quality of lime clay found in the site (and in Marrakesh generally) provided the necessary basic ingredient for trials with adobe bricks for vaulting or *pisé* techniques for walls. A special press for making bricks by hand was perfected by Mouyal, based upon the CINVA-RAM. Furthermore, a number of local masons who already possessed a limited know-how in earth construction have been trained in a variety of new or improved techniques. In all, the efforts illustrated by this house, workshops, and others have attracted the attention of local authorities for application in low-cost housing, as well as the specialised centre in Grenoble, France, called Craterre, which is particularly interested in the educational dimension for training people elsewhere.

Exterior view of the gatehouse.
Photograph: Christian Lignon.

Text courtesy of the architect. Photographs by Brian Brace Taylor unless where otherwise indicated.

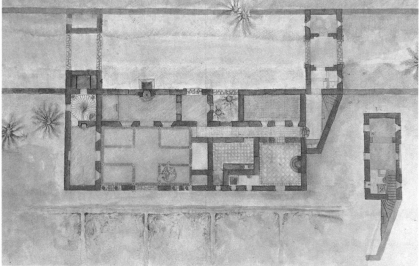

Left, top: Elevation of the west facade (top), sections and elevation of portico (middle) and longitudinal section (bottom).

Left: Ground floor plan. At right, plan of guest room over entrance portico.

Left, below: Exterior of the gatehouse with the entrance in the distance.

Below: Entrance portico to the property with guest room above.

Bottom: Entry to the gatehouse.

Right, above: Patio with living room on the right and bedroom facing.

Right: Niche, covered with a half-cupola, for sitting in the patio. Corridor to kitchen is at left, and stairs to the roof at right.

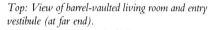

Top: *View of barrel-vaulted living room and entry vestibule (at far end).*
Above: *Raised sofa in the living room.*
Right: *Detail of cupola over the bathroom.*
Far right: *Domed bathroom and shower off the bedroom.*

Above: Bedroom.
Left: Bedroom, showing chimney, traditional lamp and mud-brick barrel vaulting.

Elie Mouyal is a Moroccan architect who studied at the Ecole des Beaux Arts in Paris. He specialises in earth construction. Mouyal currently practises in Marrakesh.

Abdelrahim Sijelmassi

Sijelmassi House, Casablanca

Project Data

*Private residence near
  Casablanca.
Client: Dr. M. Sijelmassi.
Architect: A. Sijelmassi.
Schedule: Preliminary studies
  1977, completed 1981.*

This dwelling, for a family of four, makes use of a gentle incline on a site located near the sea to organise a series of spaces inspired by traditional plans but avowedly contemporary. It has a central, covered courtyard *cum* garden space which separates reception and living rooms from sleeping quarters. The latter are situated on the higher part of the site to the east, while the living room, study, dining room, etc., are on the lower part, opening onto a small (outdoor) garden facing west.

Restrained, even austere in the architectural vocabulary that is employed, the house is nonetheless striking for the rigour of its proportions, handling of light, and sequence of linkage of spaces to one another.

Executed with conventional modern materials (i.e. reinforced concrete), it does integrate some locally-crafted elements, such as the wooden *mashrabiya* screens. Other objects of traditional origin testify to the client's reknown as an expert on Moroccan and Arab culture generally, and thus the house is a quite appropriate framework for these books and objects.

View from the seating area towards pool and pergola in the garden. The symmetry here recalls the traditional Moroccan riad.

Text and plan courtesy of the architect. Photographs by Brian Brace Taylor unless where otherwise indicated.

Garden facade with pool and lattice-covered seating area. Ceramic bricks alternate with rough bricks for paving around pool.

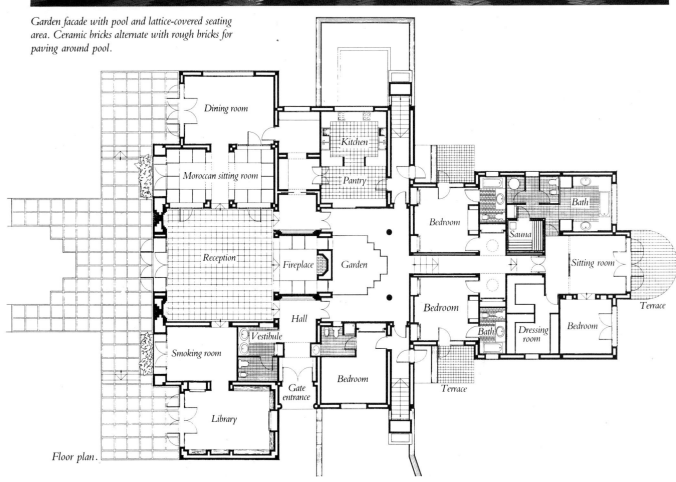

Floor plan.

Left, top: Central living room and fireplace/sitting alcove. To the right is the entrance vestibule, to the left, doorway to the covered courtyard cum garden separating public areas from bedrooms.
Photograph: M. Sijelmassi.

Left, above: Central living room and view towards the dining area (far distance). Between these are more private sitting rooms behind the mashrabiya.

Left: Private sitting area off the central living room.
Top: Passageway between two private sitting rooms off the living room. Photograph: M. Sijelmassi.

Above: View from corridor between two small sitting rooms across the living room and toward the library.

Above: View from the interior of the reception room towards the terrace and pool in the garden.
Left: Dining room.
Below: Fireplace nook adjacent to the reception room.

Left: Traditional divans around one of the small sitting rooms, with windows onto the garden.
Left, below: Corridor leading onto the dining room.

Abdelrahim Sijelmassi is a Moroccan architect living in Casablanca. He taught architecture in Paris before returning to practise in his country, where he has devoted much of his endeavour to problems of housing and institutional buildings in old city contexts.

Abdel Wahed El-Wakil

Hamdy House, Cairo

The Hamdy house on Pyramid road was from the outset intended to be a minimum economic dwelling. This completely self-contained unit, 13 metres by 10 metres, consists of 120 square metres interior space (including the mezzanine) and a 30 square metre courtyard. The whole was built for 12,000 Egyptian pounds (approximately US$18,000).

Because of the compact nature of the volume, considerable use of geometry and arithmetic proportions, such as the Golden Section, was made in order to give intelligi-ble scale and proportion to the composition of spaces, their heights, the location of the fountain in the courtyard, and so on. The Hamdy house represents an altogether different exercise from the Sulaiman palace, yet demonstrates that qualitative architectural statements can also be made with modest means.

Below: Hamdy House seen from the South.
Right, top: Courtyard with the door to the lobby.
External built-in seating, niches and different levels,
give the house an intimate scale.
Right, bottom: Lobby entrance and dining area.

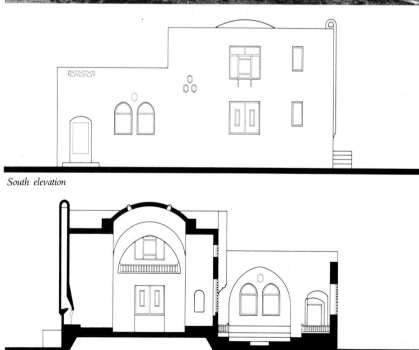

South elevation

Longitudinal section

Text by the Editors.
Photographs and
drawings courtesy of
the architect.

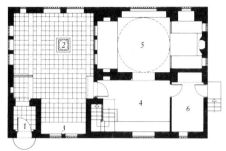

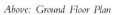

Above: Ground Floor Plan
1. Entrance   4. Lobby with dining area
2. Open courtyard   5. The Q'aa (living area)
3. Covered loggia   6. Kitchen
Above right: Mezzanine Plan
7. Sleeping loft   8. Bathroom

Below: Dining area with sleeping loft above.
Left: The domed sitting alcove with its fireplace, where interior white plastered walls contrast sharply with the brightly coloured tribal wearings and rugs.

Abdel Wahed El-Wakil is an Egyptian architect currently in private practice based in London. In 1980, his Halawa House won an Aga Khan Award for Architecture.

Abdel Wahed El-Wakil

Al Sulaiman Palace, Jeddah

The Al Sulaiman Palace, prestigiously located in the Al-Hamra district on the seashore of Jeddah, Saudi Arabia, has been much admired. The building is owned by one of the most influential families of Saudi Arabia.

"The timber merchant may think that flowers and foliage are only frivolous decorations for a tree, but he will know to his cost that if they are eliminated, the timber follows them".
— *Rabindranath Tagore*

This quotation by Tagore carries an essential truth to the propagators of material functionalism. Functionalism whose influence on modern architecture is apparent has defined utilitarian building as its most significant objective. The dull environment existing around us in cities and towns today is the result of this utilitarian approach. It is true that buildings must fulfil their immediate functions but it is imperative to recall the higher function of architecture, which is to give concrete objective expression to man's metaphysical aspirations. "Architecture is the myth of a culture, carved in stone". Its monumental buildings have provided this highest form of art.

The Sulaiman Palace was built with the intention of expressing such an ideal. If it nourishes any grandeur, it is not by means of an excessive display of wealth and pomp, but by means of arduous effort in design and craftsmanship. The Palace will have served its purpose well if it can inspire and influence the more utilitarian building-types.

Above: Al Sulaiman Palace, entrance gate and south facade.
Left: Wind catcher on the west facade, bold sculptural form-making.
Below: Site plan.
Right: Wood dome of the Sulaiman Palace, Jeddah, Saudi Arabia, seen from below.

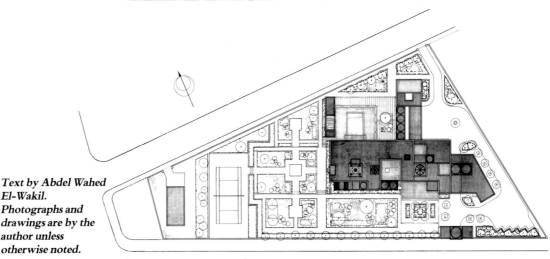

Text by Abdel Wahed El-Wakil. Photographs and drawings are by the author unless otherwise noted.

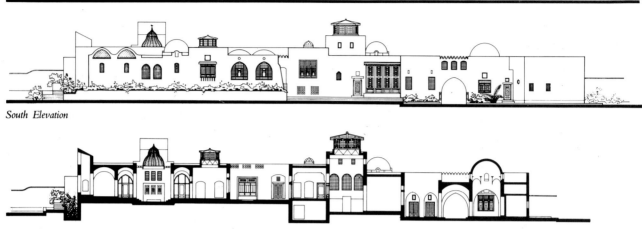

South Elevation

Longitudinal Section

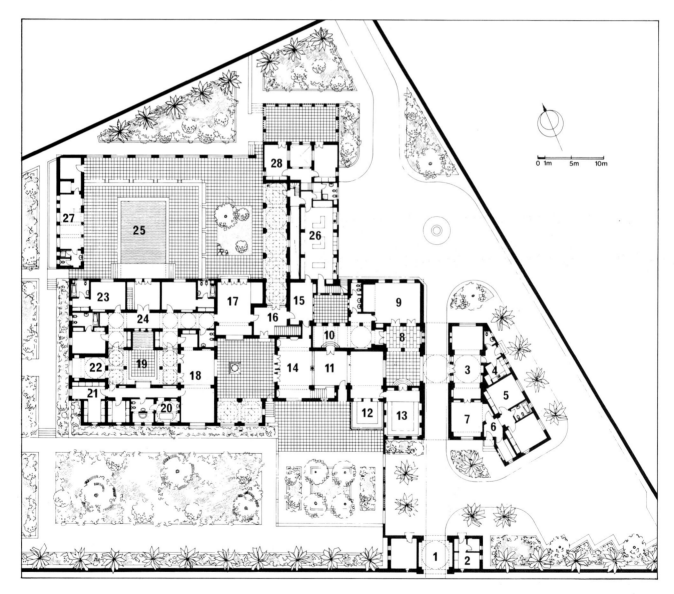

Ground Floor Plan

1. Entrance portico	6. Entry	11. Q'aa	16. Lobby	21. Dressing	26. Kitchen
2. Doorman	7. Living room	12. Roshan	17. Family room	22. Pergola	27. Pergola
3. Majlis	8. Main Entrance	13. Salamlik	18. Master bedroom	23. Bedroom	28. Servants' quarters
4. Kitchen	9. Library	14. Dining room	19. Atrium	24. Bridge/Gallery	
5. Bedroom	10. Gallery	15. Pantry	20. Bath	25. Swimming pool	

from nearby villages to visit the Sheikh) which are still a traditional aspect of Saudi culture. This hall can be integrated to the guest living room to form a larger reception space. The guest house has a separate kitchenette and can be totally independent from the main house, and can be used as separate accommodation for the younger generation of the household.

As the space for this added wing was confined within the existing internal vehicle driveways, use was made of an old design technique: aligning the elevation walls with the streets and disposing of the rooms inside accordingly, filling in spaces where necessary. This solution was often used in the old irregular street patterns and especially in Mosques where the buildings were aligned with the street whilst the prayer space was directed towards Mecca, creating interesting solutions through the reconciliation of such irregularities.

The bent entrance was a typical design characteristic in the old Arab-Islamic house by which the outside was cut off from the inside. This type of approach into the house is in complete opposition to the classical western design solution of having a direct axial entrance.

The approach by car from the covered driveway leads into an entrance courtyard which is flanked on the right by an *Iwan* (arcaded loggia) leading to the main entrance hall of the Palace. The courtyard itself provides three different entrances: the main one to the house, the second directly to the *Salamlik* (Men's Lounge) and the third, which gives direct access to the client's office and library. This offers the flexibility of using the *Salamlik* and the owner's office together with the *Majlis* without disturbing the privacy of the house; and it also allows the former rooms to be used directly from within the house.

One of my basic design principles in architecture is always to try to have access to a building in a central position. In the Sulaiman Palace this rule was broken because of the need to keep vehicle access on one side of the building: entering from the narrow east side of the building caused several problems. One of these was to articulate and break the extended longitudinal procession gallery. This was done by subdividing the entrance hall vertically by the use of different ceiling heights and floor treatments. The entrance hall is covered by a dome followed by a series of three vaults giving visual direction towards the main reception area on one side and to a small landscaped patio on the other, from which light filters through coloured glass windows above. The ceiling height drops to

The 'majlis' or reception hall with its traditional layout and differentiation of levels is still used in the same way as it was in the past.

mere door height to allow a bridge between the kitchen and dining room — thereby avoiding the crossing of circulation between the two, to cut through the main procession gallery. Access from the garage to the main entrance hall is possible through the small patio leading to an entrance under the bridge. Directly below that bridge, or connecting passage, ascending stairs lead to the central lobby separating the private areas of the house from the public areas.

The kitchen is above the car parks and is central to all areas including the main dining lounge, the family room for informal dining, the main courtyard, and the swimming pool courtyard.

The bedrooms, in the private quarters, are reached through the family room which overlooks both courtyards and is basically the meeting area of the house.

There is an open atrium in the centre of the private areas which has one loggia overlooking the garden and another leading to a small pool that connects to the swimming pool by means of a waterway. The inhabitants can go directly from their bedrooms to the atrium and swim through to the swimming pool outside the house. The atrium is shaded by means of a trellised wood-domed structure which has two wind catchers in the direction of the prevailing winds providing thermal comfort by natural means of ventilation.

The traditional use of *Mashrabiyas* (wood screens) was applied to fenestration in order to provide the functional aspects of shading and at the same time incorporating aesthetic aspects of ornamental design and craftsmanship.

Wooden lanterns, or raised domes which allow in light, another traditional element, were used in the main reception hall and master bedroom to give proper diffusion of light. The lanterns also had the further function of providing natural ventilation. Fine craftsmen fashioned doors which were panelled with geometric patterns. Many of the interior elements such as doors, niches and ceramics were restored antiques. This was intentional; its purpose was to give the place a sense of time; a dimension which is lacking in newly-made objects. Ceramics were also designed to enhance certain walls. The marble floors introduced a further dimension to design. The pattern used for the flooring was inspired from the traditional Islamic houses in Egypt.

Far left: The family living area pergola to the west with its wind-catcher.
Above: The south facade at sunset.
Left: Changing light and shadows accentuate different forms throughout the day.
Photographs: Hasan-Uddin Khan.

The client

The client, Sheikh Ahmed Al Abdullah Al Sulaiman was born in the late 1930s, and married at the early age of 19, whilst studying Business Management at a Californian University in U.S.A.

He was born of a generation that experienced the passing of the Bedouin culture and life, which in the last two decades was being increasingly influenced by the impact of modern technology. This overwhelming process of change disrupted many aspects of traditional social life and of the physical environment. The inborn 'Sense of Place' was fading beyond recognition. Ahmed Sulaiman, son of the late Prime Minister Sheikh Abdullah Al Sulaiman, who was one of the founders of Saudi Arabia, looked back with nostalgia at the environment of his childhood which was turning from reality to memory.

In 1972, he decided to build for himself, his wife and two children a house on a plot of land he had acquired in new Jeddah. He had obtained a design whilst in California several years earlier. He approached me with his Californian design and asked me to give it a 'touch of Arabesque'; something to make it look Moorish. I refused and so we began over again from scratch, with a different design philosophy.

Left: Door to the main entrance hall. The door typically from old Jeddah has been restored.
Bottom, left: Detail, wooden cupola.
Below: Replica of an old Islamic lamp from the Cairo Museum. The lamp is 2.5 metres high and hangs in the majlis.

A screened-in porch,
Roshan, *provides shade,*
privacy and filters the light to
the Q'aa.

on the Al Sulaiman Palace:
" ... architectural intrigue".

This attractive mansion is often admired and praised by most laymen. The architect of the mansion shows here his appreciation of, and sentimentality with, the traditional architecture of the Islamic world. For example, the extreme whiteness of the external wall surfaces reflects the traditional colour of all residential and public buildings of old Jeddah. Similarly, the extensive use of the wooden balconies and latticework *mashrabiyas* is borrowed directly from the traditional Jeddah Architecture. Those two features however can be found in areas throughout the Islamic world.

The architect did not confine himself to one or two schools of architecture. When viewing the building, one discovers that there is a disparate amalgamation of bits and pieces of architectural features from various Islamic Schools, Egyptian Mamlūk, Andalusian, Indian and Hijazi; yet interestingly arranged.

But because of the disparity of such architectonic features, one feels that the architect was consciously and forcibly infusing elements in order to achieve architectural expression and intrigue. The inevitable result is the subtle loss of control on architectural order in the appearance of the mansion, so that the informed critic cannot help but wonder whether he is observing a dignified residence or a playful palace in fairy-tale!

One thing has to be said however; the architect's imagination has helped him to design a building worthy of interest and study; a mansion about which many people talk and debate.

Dr. Abdulla Y. Bokhari
Jeddah, March 1981

Jafar Tukan

Villa Rizk, Amman

Project Data

A house on three levels:
living rooms, studio, three
bedrooms and a guest suite.
Owner: Mr. & Mrs. Rizk.
Completion: 1980
Total area: 870 square
metres.
Contractor: Sadik Hanna.
Materials: Local stone.

This is one of Tukan's earliest houses in Amman. The projection of the masses emphasises the various rooms within the house. An important feature in this villa, which occupies a corner site, are the arched recessed windows incorporating planters. The client and his artist wife, who gave Tukan a free hand, have complimented the concept of the house through their treatment of the interior which is both dramatic and boldly original. Taken as a whole, this villa is perhaps the most successful of Tukan's residential architecture.

Top: The villa viewed from the street.
Above: The rear of the villa. The upstairs bedrooms have recessed windows protected from the sun and planters which add colour and contrast with the hard stone surfaces.
Right: The formal living room decorated by the owners mixes European furniture with oriental rugs and fabrics.

Text by Akram Abu Hamdan.
Photographs courtesy of the architect.

Jafar Tukan is the most established figure on the Jordanian architectural scene. He lives in Amman.

Nail Cakirhan

Inkaya House, Muğla

Project Data

Location: A weekend cottage in Akyaka Village, Muğla, Turkey.
Client: Dr. Minu Inkaya.
Designer: Nail Cakirhan.
Floor area: 65 square metres (not including eaves).
Cost: 225000 TL (US$15,000)
Date of construction: From June to November 1975. (Occupied in December 1975).
Construction: Traditional timber-frame.

The Minu Inkaya house in rural Turkey was designed by a writer-turned-master builder, Mr. Nail Cakirhan, on 450 square metres of land quite near to his own house which he also designed and built in the same traditional style. Having admired and studied the local wooden house architecture of his native region along the Southern Aegean Coast, Mr. Cakirhan has been instrumental in reviving a demand for high quality carpentry evident in these houses. Conceived for a single woman medical doctor of modest income (she has no private practice but works in public health), the plan reflects the compactness and efficient organisation desired of an abode for peaceful, contemplative relaxation in natural surroundings.

Several local master carpenters constructed, under Mr. Cakirhan's direction after a simple working sketch had been transferred to the ground, a wooden frame structure set upon masonry foundations. The white-washed walls are constituted by brick infill, and the floors and ornamental ceiling are of wood.

The interior space is essentially that of a one-room, multi-purpose living environment, for eating, sleeping and working. This is extended outwards, if you will, along the southern facade by a porch with a bay-like shape, giving additional living space. The main room is rectangular with the corners cut off at 45 degrees, providing windows and thus enhanced ventilation and view. At each end of the longitudinal axis of the living room there is a sleeping alcove, separated from the main room by orna-

mented wooden columns and arches. To provide autonomy, each alcove has a side-board, bookshelves and a cupboard — all accessible from within the alcove. Storage space is provided in trunk-like wooden couches and in the spaces above the alcoves that are closed off by carved wooden gratings. Finally, there is the traditional serpenç, or continuous shelf that runs around the walls, doors, and windows and upon which objects are stored or displayed. Apart from two built-in wooden couches there is no other furniture — just rugs and cushions.

Symmetrically opposite the porch and having the same shape in plan, is an enclosed space comprising the kitchen and bathroom. The doors to these two separate rooms are located on either side of the chimney.

The Minu Inkaya house, while reflecting the typology of local domestic architecture in different ways, is nevertheless an adaptation of such elements to the personal needs and desires of the client. Simplicity and elegance characterise the interior spaces, where the white-washed walls contrast with the warmness of the wood finishing and elaborately carved ceiling. Mr. Cakirhan, through his determination and devotion to the cause of reviving local building crafts, has demonstrated that high quality yet economical alternatives to the prevailing reinforced concrete construction do exist and are rich in innovative potential.

Below: Exterior view of the M. Inkaya house, located near Nail Cakirhan's own house.
Right: View of the porch pergola from inside the house.
Photographs: R. Gunay/AKAA.

Text by Brian Taylor. Photographs by Reha Gunay, courtesy Aga Khan Award for Architecture.

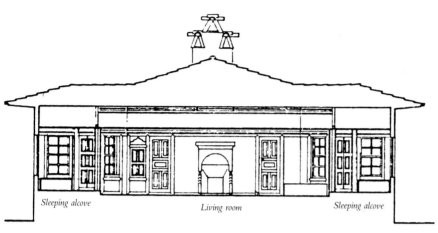

Sleeping alcove   Living room   Sleeping alcove

Section

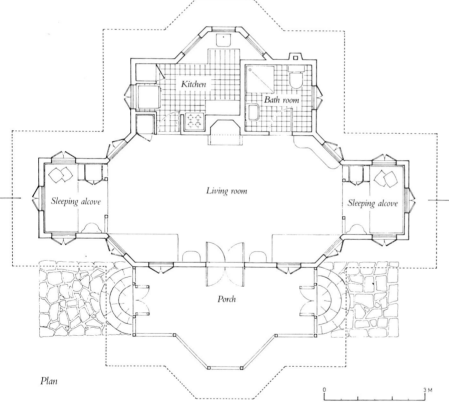

Kitchen

Bath room

Sleeping alcove   Living room   Sleeping alcove

Porch

Plan

0   3 M

Minu Inkaya, a medical doctor and close friend of the Cakirhans, works only in state hospitals.

Left: Living room with sleeping alcove at each end of the room. The pine ceiling was executed by local carpenters following the designs of Nail Çakirhan. Photograph: R. Gunay/AKAA.

Nail Cakirhan was a poet and writer before becoming a self-educated architect/builder. Having studied and worked with local craftsmen, he has built eighteen houses in the village of Akyaka alone since he designed his own residence in 1970.

Ahmet Gülgönen

Gülgönen House, Istanbul

This house, built in 1981 on the Anatolian side of the Bosphorus, occupies an extraordinary site: it is situated on a steep slope overlooking the water, with a forest behind it. The programme for the house included two apartments, one larger and one smaller unit. However, the means for separating one from the other are such that rooms may be temporarily attached to an apartment as use dictates. The arrangement of the two apartments under the same roof, giving the image of a large house derives from the fact that the two units were originally designed for two branches of the same, extended family. Therefore, a unified whole is expressed rather than an attempt at diversity.

Organisation of the interior spaces has consciously benefitted from the slope of the site, by providing the entrance to the smaller apartment on the lowest of three levels. It is then connected to two other rooms on the second and third levels. The entrance to the main house is located on the second level. Here the central space with the living and dining rooms form a spatial continuum in which each of the two functions is articulated.

The living room is two storeys high, offering views to the sky and the surrounding landscape while entertaining a visual relationship with the upper living room. At the third floor level are the bedrooms and balconies.

The main spaces of the second floor, along the principal axis of the house, are truly open to the surrounding environment. This transparency sought by the designer emphasises that the house can share the unique dual qualities of Bosphorus and forest from its location. Such a solution also makes the dimensions of the house seem more spacious, opening to nature visually but also climatically: an agreeable cross ventilation is obtainable in summer.

South facade. Irregular volumetry reflects transition from square to octogonal plan.

**Text by Brian Brace Taylor.
Photographs and drawings courtesy of the architect.**

In plan, this house takes its inspiration from historical examples of 19th century house-types found along the Bosphoros. The architect did not search for artificial similarities, decorative or otherwise, with old Turkish dwellings. Rather the links with the past are conceptual, in terms of spatial organisation: the central plan is typical of many Turkish houses, particularly those which Professor Sedad Eldem has characterised as the "inner hall" type, with an axial disposition of common spaces.

An important characteristic of this house is its three-dimensionality. The plan is transformed as one passes from one level to the next: at the lower level, the plan is cruciform, being transformed successively into a square and then an octagon, with a system of bow windows, at the upper level. This kind of transformation of plans and the use of bow windows are typical of Turkish domestic architecture. The conception of spaces is thus intimately related to the geometry in this particular dwelling, where the plan of each floor is generated from·the central space. An overall unity is created among smaller articulated spaces, or individual rooms and common spaces, because of this relationship space-geometry.

The development of articulated spaces around a central space has been a recurrent theme in earlier work by this architect. In each instance, however, the context and function of the building has brought about different meanings for the central space. A certain dialectical relationship evolved between inner hall and peripheral spaces. In this recent house, the inner hall is the generating element for the spaces that surround it, while symbolically expressing the intimacy and unity of family life. (The corollary is, of course, the various rooms for *individual* activity.)

This recent variation on a conceptual theme ought to be compared with the school designed and built with the aid of M.E.T.U. students in the village of Nigde (Cappadocchia, central Anatolia) where the central space is essentially a distribution space for the classrooms. Its relative autonomy, as a multi-functional space with respect to the classrooms, is expressed by its skylight, under which children meet, play and pass back and forth between interior and exterior. Still another example but of a different sort altogether is the museum at Gallipoli which has an open interior courtyard, surrounded by a series of exhibition spaces. (These have a linear continuity also). This courtyard serves as a transition space between inner spaces and the outside. It expresses the contrast between the vastness

Right, above: Living room with its bent-wood furniture.
Right: View of the double height space with an outdoor verandah upstairs and the living area below.

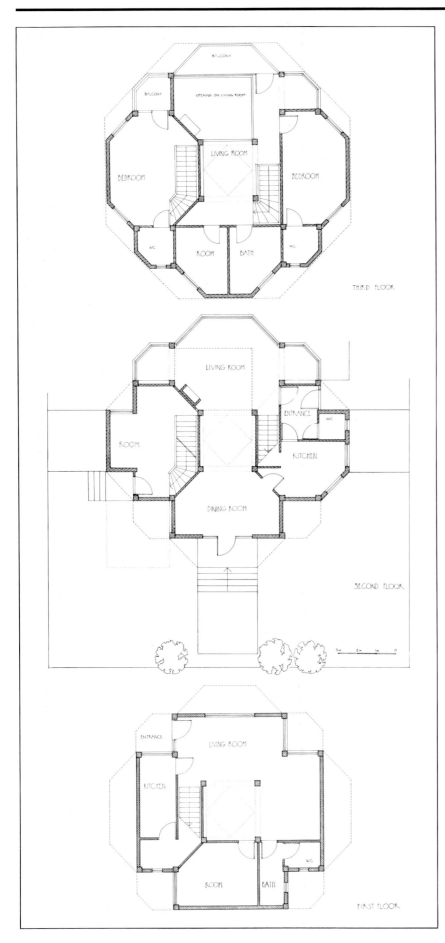

THIRD FLOOR

SECOND FLOOR

FIRST FLOOR

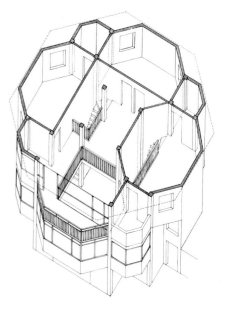

of the landscape and the perfectly dimensioned space of the museum.

These examples demonstrate how a particular conception of space and one of its elements — the central space — can be used in different building-types today. This notion, deeply-rooted in history, responds to spiritual needs, both individual and collective, that seek expression visually and spatially in centrally-oriented realms.

Left: Plans of first, second and third floors. Smaller first floor apartment has cruciform plan with square central hall, and stairs to second-floor room. Entrance to main house is on second level. Central square space continues through two floors. Overall shape of the volume becomes an octagon at upper level.

Top: Axonometric drawing depicting central hall, peripheral rooms and terraces.

Below: Typical 19th century Turkish house plan which inspired the Gulgonen residence. Parallels are with the central hall plan, symmetrical stairs, and bow windows.

Right: Southwest facade, with entrance to lower apartment. Stairs lead to garden behind the house.

Overleaf: View from third floor down into main living room.

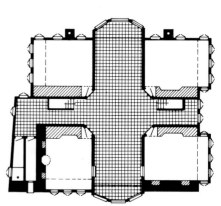

Left: Double height space with bow window and alcoves, and view onto the Bosphorus.
Above: Main entry, looking through dining room to living room. Garden behind the house is reflected in windows.
Left: Garden with antique fountain behind the house.

Ahmet Gülgönen was born in Ankara, Turkey and educated at M.E.T.U. before taking a Master's degree in the U.S.A. with the architect Louis Kahn. He now lives and practises in France but continues to do projects abroad, including studies for a new philharmonic hall in Istanbul.

Architect's Residence, Karachi

Project Data

Location: Khaliquzzaman
Road, Karachi, Pakistan.
Client and architect: Habib
Fida Ali, the Pakistani
architect and interior
designer remodelled this
house for himself.
Completion: May 1983.
Construction: Re-design of a
19th Century stone house
with terracotta tiled roof,
plastered and painted walls
and ceilings and hardwood
floors.

This house, one of the few remaining in Karachi from the British colonial era, has been Habib Fida Ali's residence since the mid-1960's. From time to time the architect, a bachelor, has re-decorated it, changing and adapting it to his life-style. The house, last re-done in 1974, was featured both in *Architectural Digest* and *MIMAR*.

In 1983 Fida Ali extensively remodelled the building, including the upper storey for the first time, to reflect his somewhat spartan, simple and elegant tastes. His calculated placing of objects and furniture, the creation of "activity zones," vistas, nooks and crannies, illustrates the use of the house as a backdrop for a small collection of art objects.

The combination of modern conveniences; fans and air-conditioning, new furniture, with the high-ceiling rooms, old teak floors and arched doorways, reflects his westernised life-style, yet gives the house a feeling of peace in the heart of the busy city.

At a time when affluent Pakistanis are looking for "modern architecture," it is refreshing to see someone use an old building so well for contemporary living.

Above: The entrance to the house is shaded by old trees.
Below: A seating alcove off the living room. The sofa is covered in local raw silk and the original bent wood chairs were picked up in a Karachi junk market. The rug is an old caucasian. The coloured glass in the windows is an original feature of such houses, as are the hardwood floors.
Right: The living room. The paintings are Mughal miniatures in brass frames. The Gandhara sculpture on the mantlepiece is of the 2nd Century.

**Text by the Editors.
Photographs by Farooq Turab.
Drawings courtesy of the architect.**

Above: Hand-blocked ajrak cloth panels (designed by the architect) line the walls of the thematic black and white dining room.

Right: The verandah is furnished in white Sindhi furniture; Dutch hanging lamps and an old chest stands on the refinished teak floors.

Above: The stark black and white dining room. The walls are covered in silk hand-blocked panels created by Noorjehan Bilgrami, adapting an age-old ajrak design. Left: Detail of an ajrak panel.

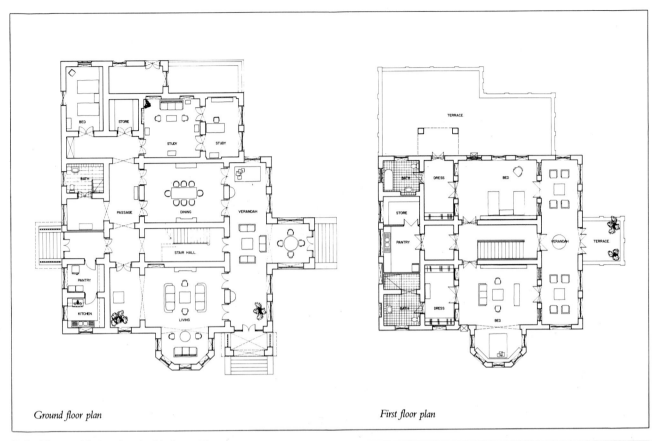

Ground floor plan   First floor plan

Right: The verandah along the side of the house. The furniture is made out of old carved, head and foot boards of beds, painted white. The Dutch hanging oil lamps have been electrified.

Far left: Fida Ali's study is carpeted and comfortable, giving a feeling of warmth. The wall hanging, a fine Senna gelim in delicate glowing colours with the so-called Heratic pattern, is from Iran. The sofas are covered in local cotton, with silk cushions. The old Arab chest is inlaid in mother-of-pearl. The silk rug on the carpet is Afghani.
Left: The passage has a beautifully carved old almirah. On the floor is a gelim from the south of Iran.
Left, below: The spartan bedroom is in pale colours, accentuated by an antique Kashan carpet.

Habib Fida Ali established his office since 1965 in Karachi where he continues to live and work. Today he is one of Pakistan's best-known architects.

Habib Fida Ali

17th Street House, Karachi

Project Data

*House in Defence Housing
  Society, Karachi.
Owner: Habib Fida Ali.
Design Team: H. Fida Ali,
  M. Kalam Baig.
Completion: June 1979.*

From the mid-1970's the direction of Fida Ali's designs started to change. He experimented with his own house, which though not built for himself (it is rented to an embassy), incorporates several of his recent ideas on house design. (Note how different this building is from the earlier Kabrajee House which is a typical example of the architect's 1960's and 1970's buildings.)

The site for the 17th Street House was a long and narrow rectangle (60 feet × 120 feet) with residential plots on both the north and south sides. The house has been oriented toward the prevailing breezes, with the living areas in the front and the services to the rear. The bedrooms, with their own small utility area, are on the first floor. The Master Bedroom upstairs commands a view across the lawn, as well as into the court from a private terrace. The ground floor is basically an open plan wrapped around an interior court. The staircase window is

shaded by a simple but dramatic screen of vertical slats of wood, painted white.

The architect has retained a clarity of line in the design and has emphasised one **organisational** element — the central courtyard. He avoided exterior add-ons, such as the ledges or sun-shades, that wrap around most of the Karachi houses. His solution was to cantilever the top floor over the ground floor and then set back both windows and unit air-conditioners. In the interior, the spaces on both sides of these recesses became convenient built-in storage niches.

Much of Karachi's urban landscape is such a multi-hued and elaborate concoction, it is ironical that the uncluttered facade of this house makes it appear almost alien by contrast.

**Text by Sabir Khan and
Hasan-Uddin Khan.
Photographs courtesy
of Timothy Hursley.
Drawings courtesy of
the architect.**

Above: The entrance driveway to the house cuts into the plot to allow for a more central approach to the front door and also creates a private garden in the front.
Left: The central courtyard spills out to a narrow side garden. The free standing wall, at centre, is for privacy.

The house seen from the side shows a simple profile sloping towards the front. The vertical wood slats protect the staircase and other windows from the sun.

Right: The entry courtyard, lit as night falls, leads the visitor to the main entrance to the house. To the left is the living room which overlooks the garden.

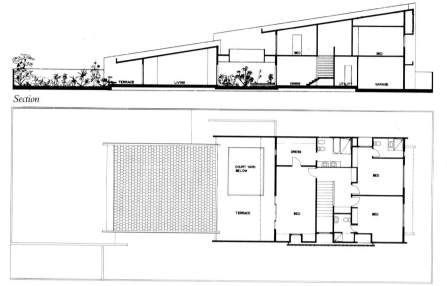

Section

First floor plan

0 1   5m

Ground floor plan

Yasmeen Lari

Lari House, Karachi

The site which is approximately 1505 square metres has a drop of sixteen feet (5 metres) across it. The house sits at the edge of the drop and has a twenty foot (6 metres) cantilevered verandah which gives a dramatic view of the garden below. The house is a reinforced concrete framed structure with brick facing.

The structure is based on a four foot (1.2 metres) grid with exposed beams supporting pyramids of asbestos cement. Some of these have openings which act as wind catchers, which is a traditional element that is used in this region to encourage air circulation.

The internal layout itself is based on an open plan, except for the bedrooms. The overall design allows for a continuous flow of breeze throughout.

Text complied by MIMAR's editors. Drawings and photographs courtesy of Lari Associates.

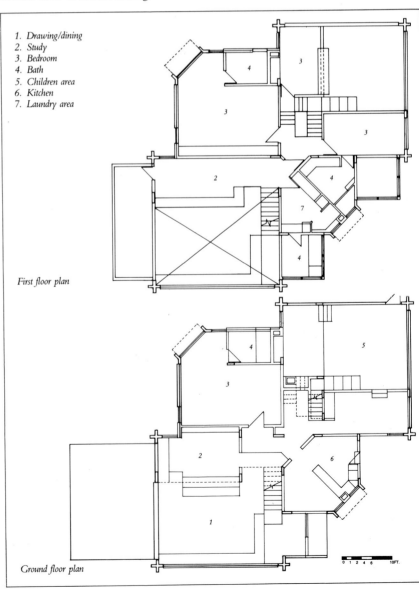

1. Drawing/dining
2. Study
3. Bedroom
4. Bath
5. Children area
6. Kitchen
7. Laundry area

First floor plan

Ground floor plan

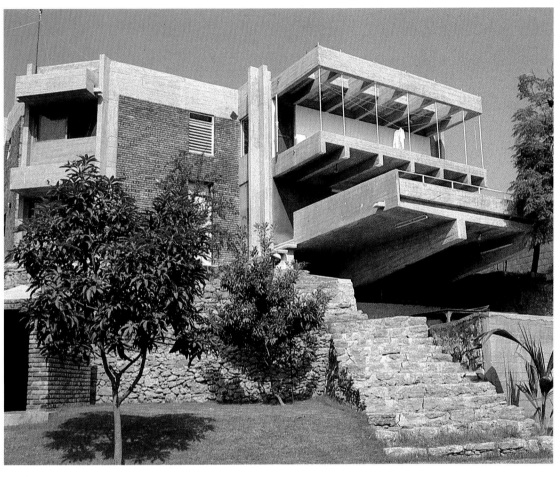

Yasmeen Lari is a Pakistani architect in private practice in Karachi.

77

Satish Gujral

Belgian Embassy, New Delhi

Project Data

Client: Government of
  Belgium.
Designer: Satish Gujral.
Land: 5 acres (approx. 2
  hectares).
Covered area: 4000 square
  metres.
Construction period: 3 years
  (1980-1983).
Cost: US$2 million.

Aim

The project was commissioned by the Belgian Government for housing its Chancery, the ambassador's residence and servant quarters. The design was laid down along a central east-west axis, to which a Chancellor's residence and a sunken tennis court were added later.

Concept

A standard dictionary defines organic as "characterised by co-relation and co-operation of parts; organised by laws like those of life, not mechanical; depending on structural; fundamental." Thus organic architecture is design which places emphasis on the direct use of materials,

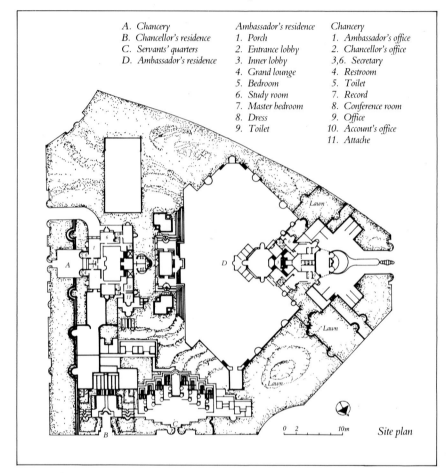

A. Chancery
B. Chancellor's residence
C. Servants' quarters
D. Ambassador's residence

Ambassador's residence
1. Porch
2. Entrance lobby
3. Inner lobby
4. Grand lounge
5. Bedroom
6. Study room
7. Master bedroom
8. Dress
9. Toilet

Chancery
1. Ambassador's office
2. Chancellor's office
3,6. Secretary
4. Restroom
5. Toilet
7. Record
8. Conference room
9. Office
10. Account's office
11. Attache

Site plan

Text and photographs
by Satish Gujral.

Left, bottom: Living room of the residence.
Above: The ambassador's residence at night.

the exposure of their surfaces, and an independence of all parts of the structure with one another, as well as the sum total of parts and its relationship to the environmental setting. "Organic" therefore implies logical and natural growth, a harmony within the structure and a sense of belonging evident in the relationship of the building.

I had been fortunate, in a way, that the requirements were few as compared to the size of the site. This enabled me to place each building in a manner that they were all independent yet tied together by series of passages and landscape, which is the binding force. The entire landscaping was man-made since the existing site was flat. This was necessary since it was the only natural solution to integrate the buildings. Also due to the size of the site, it was important to create private, semi-private areas, in a way not to impose on the built form. The land rises in parts forming upper level gardens, gets cut out as parts forming tennis courts, also helps to conceal the servant quarters and at the same time protects them against the Delhi sun. Also, local materials were chosen and left exposed to create an organic

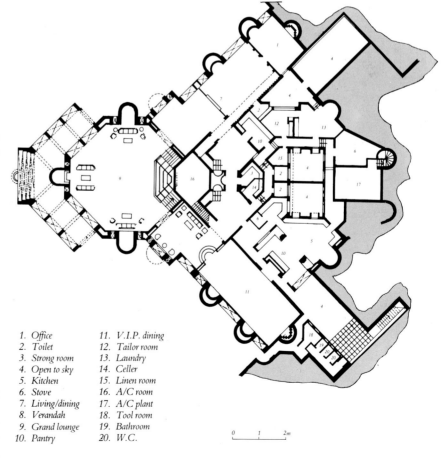

1. Office	11. V.I.P. dining
2. Toilet	12. Tailor room
3. Strong room	13. Laundry
4. Open to sky	14. Celler
5. Kitchen	15. Linen room
6. Stove	16. A/C room
7. Living/dining	17. A/C plant
8. Verandah	18. Tool room
9. Grand lounge	19. Bathroom
10. Pantry	20. W.C.

Ground floor plan, residence.

Left: Entry to the living room of ambassador's residence.
Above: Dining-room of ambassador's residence.
Right: Residence kitchen.

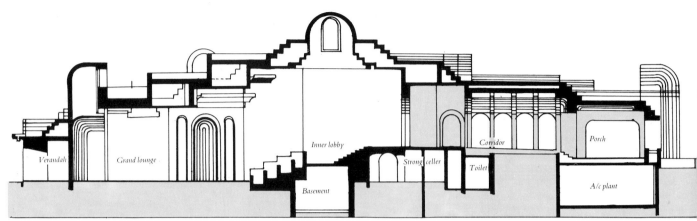

Section, ambassador's residence.

ambience-born from things instead of super imposing on them.

I must also admit that it was fortunate for me to be able to build this project myself on a turn-key basis, which gave me a tremendous opportunity to re-assess and re-design during the process of construction. The final result evolved through discriminative and constant choices while actively engaged. Since creative action, which makes up a work of art, is dependent upon an active involvement of the individual during the working process, flexibility is essential to taking advantage of newly-discovered relationships which may determine new responses or intuitions that frequently change the initial visualisation.

As far as the style is concerned, it would be difficult to categorise. I have an open mind towards history that foreshadows the post-modernist attitude. The difference doesn't come from the repetition, but from the initial removal compensated for by an endless reapproaching. Historical knowledge is essential for every architect. But if it is true knowledge, it never leads to historicism. An artist is constantly absorbing all that is around him. He then juxtaposes it in his mind to come out with a creation that has his own interpretation, his own style.

Satish Gujral was born in December 1925. He lives and works in New Delhi and is one of the founders of contemporary School of Indian Art. His sculptures and paintings are included in major collections of the world and he is thrice winner of National Award for painting and sculpture.

The Garden, Lunuganga

Project Data

Lunugaga Estate, House and Garden
Site: 25 acres on Dedduwa Lake, Sri Lanka
Client: The architect
Date: Begun in 1920 and ongoing

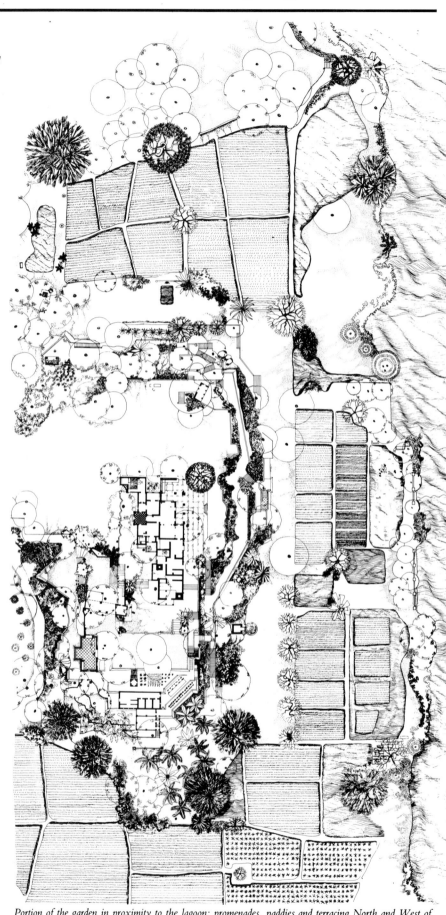

Text by Brian Brace Taylor.
Photographs and drawings courtesy of the architect unless otherwise noted.

Portion of the garden in proximity to the lagoon: promenades, paddies and terracing North and West of the house.

The site of this idyllic retreat is a former rubber plantation, with an existing house, purchased in 1949 — before Geoffrey Bawa had actually decided to become an architect. It may even have been the catalyst that determined him to return to England and to take a degree in design. Located on a backwater of the Bentota river, south of Colombo, the garden and the house have been a constant focus of the architect's energies; making incremental additions to the abode, often with materials recovered from demolished old structures; shaping and reshaping the garden as the spirit moved him through cutting of the wildly luxurious vegetation and selective planting. The garden is for all intents and purposes an extension of the rooms of the dwelling, containing objects, tiny pavilions, pavements and vantage points for observing a succession of spaces in continual transformation.

Top: Looking northward across the watergate.
Photograph: Milroy Perera.
Right, above: Mask of a Hindu Pan in the Lunuganga garden.
Right: South facade of the house with main entrance.
Photographs: Brian Taylor.

Sectional elevation of the house and its recent extensions.

Plan of the pavilion, hen house, and adjacent landscaping, in 1983.

Above: Guest room, a recent extension to the old house. Photograph: Brian Taylor.
Right: Interior of guest room.
Right, below: Interior of pavilion, part of the new extension.
Photographs: Hasan-Uddin Khan.

Left: Entrance steps and colonnaded portico.
Left, below: View from the porch of the house looking towards the lagoon.
Left, bottom: The main house from the west garden.
Photographs: Hasan-Uddin Khan.

Geoffrey Bawa, a Sri Lankan architect, came into the profession only in his late 30s. He is his country's best known architect and is the subject of a Mimar monograph.

Geoffrey Bawa

Architect's Residence, Colombo

Project Data

*The Architect's House,
restructuring and
rehabilitation.
Site: Bagatelle Road,
Colombo.
Acquisition of initial
portion: 1958.
Second acquisition: 1968.*

This truly remarkable dwelling is in constant evolution, having originally been not one, but four, adjacent houses. The architect was able to acquire them starting in 1958 and has unified them into a series of living spaces with numerous courtyards, lightwells and views onto the out of doors. Columns from ancient buildings now demolished find their place among other artifacts which the architect has incorporated into his residence. Partly because of the owner's particular tastes and personality, but also due to the fact that several units have been combined into one, the spaces must be experienced sequentially; each possesses a unique character and atmosphere.

Left: View from the garage down the entrance hallway.
Below: Patio with bench adjacent to central sitting room.

**Text by Brian Brace
Taylor.
Photographs courtesy
of Richard Bryant
unless otherwise noted.
Drawings courtesy of
the architect.**

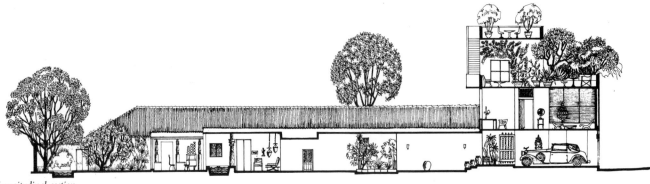

Longitudinal section.

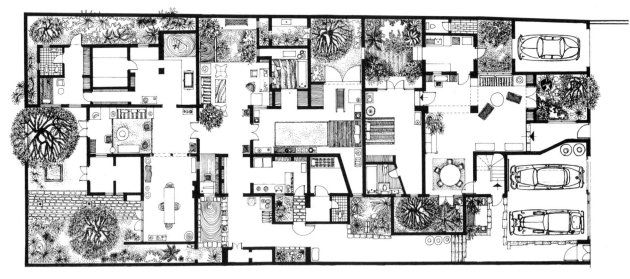

Ground floor plan.

Left: Columns at end of entrance hallway. Door painted by D. Friend.
Below: View from bedroom towards the rear garden.

Left: Decorated door to upstairs sitting room. Stairs to roof terrace.
Below: Upstairs sitting room.
Below, right: Roof terrace. Photograph: Christoph Bon.

Peter White House, Mauritius

Project Data

House, Mauritius
Programme: Transformation
of an existing sugar cane
warehouse
Client: Mr. Peter White
Architect: Edwards, Reid &
Begg, Geoffrey Bawa
Date: 1974

Originally, these two long, barrel-vaulted spaces were built and used as warehouses for sugar cane. They were purchased and Mr Bawa was commissioned by the client to transform them into a weekend house. The programme involved only a bedroom, a bathroom and a small kitchen, while the rest of the space could be utilised in a variety of ways. Outbuildings nearby were converted into guest bedrooms. The sketch drawings by the architect for this project contain numerous annotations as to potential arrangements for spaces and their use, but the two basic criteria expressed by the client were the desire for quiet solitude and the possibility for inviting large groups of people.

Exterior view of east facade.

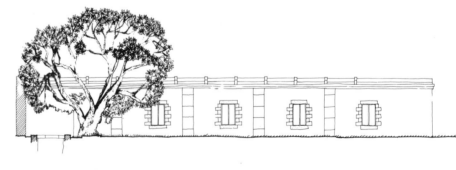

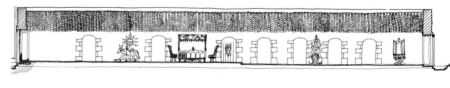

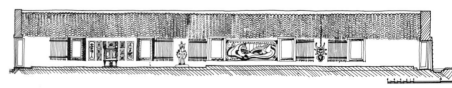

Transversal, longitudinal sections and elevation of the house.

Text by Brian Brace
Taylor.
Photographs courtesy
of Peter White.
Drawings courtesy of
the architect.

Above: Interior view of the vaulted dining room.
Right: Bedroom.

Transversal sections of the valted spaces.

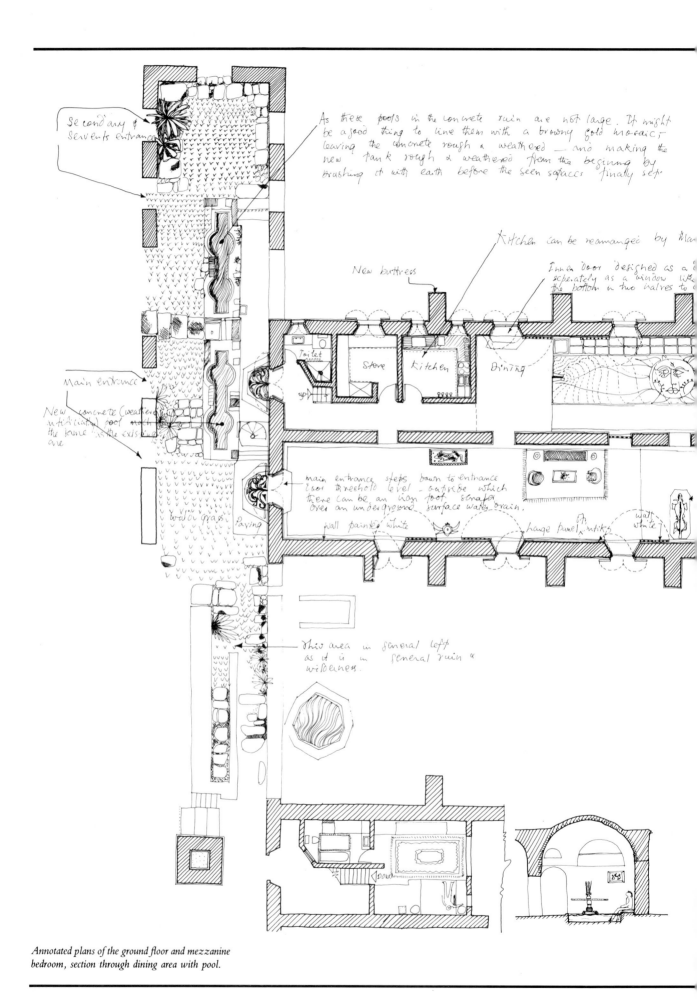

As these pools in the concrete ruin are not large. It might be a good thing to line them with a browny gold mosaic — leaving the concrete rough & weathered — and making the new tank rough & weathered from the begining by brushing it with earth before the seen surfaces finally set.

Secondary & Servants entrance

New buttress

Kitchen can be rearranged by Ma...

Inner Door designed as a... seperately as a window li... the bottom in two halves to...

Toilet

Stove

Kitchen

Dining

Main entrance

New concrete (weather... artificial... pool much... the same as the existing one

main entrance steps down to entrance & threshold level — outside which there can be an iron foot scraper over an underground surface water drain.

Lawn grass

Paving

wall painted white

large panel antiks

wall white

This area in general left as it is in general ruin & wilderness.

Annotated plans of the ground floor and mezzanine bedroom, section through dining area with pool.

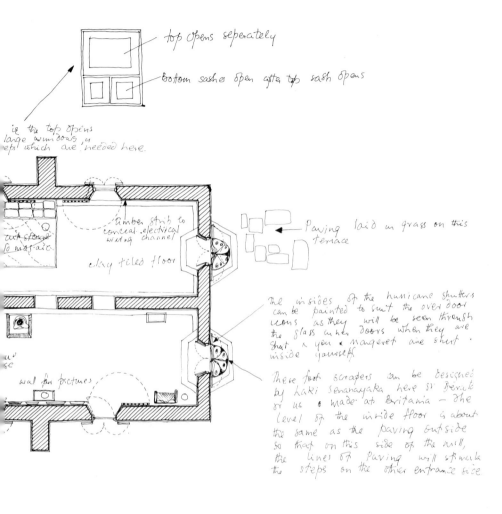

top Opens seperately

bottom sashes open after top sash opens

is the top opens
large windows, a
steps which are needed here.

timber strip to
conceal electrical
wiring channel

cut stone
to mosaic.

clay tiled floor

wall for pictures

Paving laid on grass on this
terrace

The insides of the hurricane shutters
can be painted to suit the over door
icons as they will be seen through
the glass when doors when they are
shut, & you & margaret are shut
inside yourself.

These foot scrapers can be designed
by Laki Senanayaka here St Benet's
or us & made at Britania — The
level of the inside floor is about
the same as the paving outside
so that on this side of the wall,
the lines of Paving will still mark
the steps on the other entrance side

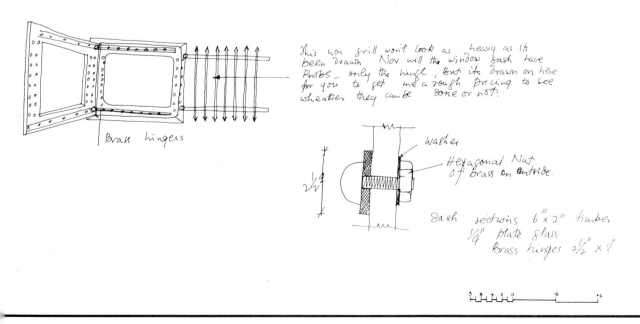

Brass hinges

This war grill won't look as heavy as its
been drawn. Nor will the window sash have
knobs — only the hinge, but its drawn on here
for you to get me a rough pricing to see
wheather they can be done or not.

Washer

Hexagonal Nut
of Brass on Outside.

2½"

Sash sections 6"x 2" timber
¼" plate glass
Brass hinges 2½" x 2"

95

Boonyawat and Pussadee Tiptus

Tiptus House, Bangkok

The Thai Spirit in Modern Technology

Studies have revealed that houses in the central region in the Early Rattanakosin Period (1782 — Present) shared certain dominant characteristics. Typically, the house was a one-storey wooden structure on stilts. Rectangular in form, it had a high-pitched roof and extended overhangs and an elevated wooden verandah. It could be a single building for young married couples, twin buildings or a group of buildings depending on the owner's wealth, social status or the number of people in the family. There were, however, many factors which contributed to the development of such characteristics.

Firstly, with the Chao Phraya River passing through the city of Bangkok, which was a low-lying area, the waterway became a major route of transportation. People, therefore, built their houses along the river and canals (klongs). Since water sometimes overflowed the banks at certain times of the year when the water level was generally high, it was necessary that houses be built on stilts as protection against floods and reptiles. When the water receded, the ground space under the

house could be used as a place for family members to do housework and to store some tools. People living on higher ground also adopted this same style of house and thus could make use of the ground space for household activities all year round.

Secondly, wood, a locally available material, was employed for the main structure. Building materials such as bamboo, thatch, mat or planks were used as wall panels. These materials were usually prefabricated and later attached to the house structure.

Thirdly, sunshine and frequent rainfalls necessitated a house with a high pitched roof and extended overhangs. This was to keep the sun and rain off the walls.

Fourthly, a house in a tropical climate had to be designed to ensure good ventilation and shade. Most daily activities were often performed in semi-outdoor spaces such as on the balcony, verandah, terrace and under the house.

Lastly, the close relations among members of a Thai family were also reflected in architecture. A single-family house normally consisted of more than

Exterior view from the south, showing pilotis with parents' bedroom above and covered patio below.

Plans and photographs courtesy of the architects/owners, Boonyawat and Pussadee Tiptus.

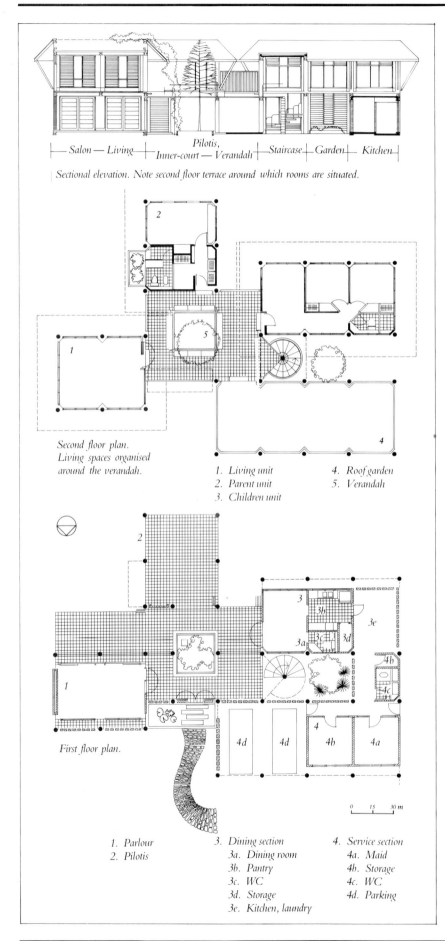

Sectional elevation. Note second floor terrace around which rooms are situated.

├ Salon ─ Living ┼ Pilotis, Inner-court ─ Verandah ┼ Staircase ┼ Garden ┼ Kitchen ┤

Second floor plan.
Living spaces organised
around the verandah.

1. Living unit   4. Roof garden
2. Parent unit   5. Verandah
3. Children unit

First floor plan.

1. Parlour   3. Dining section   4. Service section
2. Pilotis   3a. Dining room   4a. Maid
                3b. Pantry   4b. Storage
                3c. WC   4c. WC
                3d. Storage   4d. Parking
                3e. Kitchen, laundry

one unit: a sleeping unit for parents or the head of the family, another sleeping unit for children, a living unit and a kitchen. These units, though varying in size, were the same in basic form and were adjoined by a central terrace, a multi-purpose area for shared activities. On the terrace, potted plants were placed and a trellis for climbing plants could be erected to provide shade and coolness. At that time, Thai families were of an extended type, that is, married children still lived with their parents, and another unit for a married son or daughter could be added and adjoined to the central terrace, an extension which allowed the family to be together while still maintaining privacy.

These dominant characteristics were undeniably the result of a gradual development of the basic form of a Thai dwelling over the years; the characteristics were apparently suited to the climate and ways of living of the people. However, houses in Thailand nowadays have tended to develop towards a more "international style" due to the influence of Western architecture, advanced technology and a great variety of construction materials. Consequently, one rarely sees architects or house owners who revert to the traditional form of the dwelling house, resulting in the disruption of the long-developed house style.

Built in 1982, this house was an attempt to apply the design concepts of the traditional Thai dwelling in terms of atmosphere, space arrangement and grouping of buildings to modern living and technology. The architects, while considering the requirements of the occupants, made an attempt to incorporate the major characteristics of the traditional house in his design. The requirements of the occupants were:

• suitability for the tropical climate
• provision for privacy by dividing the house into separate units with a common area for all
• equal use of outdoor, semi-outdoor and indoor spaces
• efficient utilisation of spaces
• durability and economy
• flexibility for future extension
• conservation of existing large trees at the site

In an effort to design a house that answered these requirements, the architects had done a number of things.

To design a house that is suitable for the tropical climate, the architects

Right: Interior of the parlour.

Right: Entry as seen from the exterior.
Below: View of the entrance seen from the interior.
Bottom: Lower level courtyard and verandah on second floor.

Right: Sitting area on the first floor next to the main entrance of the house.
Below: View of the first floor courtyard (at left) rising through the centre of the house, with stairs to upper floor.

living unit and a kitchen together with a service area. (The rooftop of this part is a deck with a trellis.) These units are adjoined by a central terrace.

To utilise both indoor and outdoor space equally, the architects arranged outdoor and semi-outdoor spaces as multipurpose areas. Areas which have natural air flow like the terrace, deck, verandah as well as the ground space can be best used for leisurely sittings, doing some housework, and receiving friends.

In order to utilise space most efficiently, the architect designed only for the minimum, i.e. the size of each room is adequate for functional use with no space wasted. As for multi-purpose areas where both privacy and comfort are needed, stripped breathing walls have been used, thus allowing free air flow and affording privacy without making one feel confined at the same time.

Durability and economy were achieved by the use of low-cost local materials including sun-dried handmade brick, handmade terracotta, terracotta roof tiles and handmade glazed ceramic tiles. Furthermore, prefabricated materials of the same module were used. With precast concrete beams and floors, construction cost and time could be saved and quality controlled. The walling was of prefabricated lath and plaster panel in wooden frames of the same modular, similar to the use of prefabricated traditional, patterned, wooden panels in the past. Such light-weight materials evidently made construction easier and quicker.

Instead of a high pitched roof of the traditional house, a flat concrete roof was employed so as to provide space on the rooftop for the installation of mechanical equipment such as air-conditioning compressor, solar cell arrays, etc. A ceiling was put up to block heat radiation from concrete roof to the interior.

As a provision for extension in the future, the architects designed the house as a group of units so that a married child and his or her family could occupy one unit while sharing common areas with the rest. Besides, if need be, an addition could be made in areas which are now the deck and the ground space.

To conserve as many existing trees as possible, the buildings were located in the front part of the land leaving a rain tree, banana and coconut trees undisturbed.

This house won a gold medal award for residential building from the Association of Siamese Architects in 1984.

arranged it in such a way that most areas faced southerly and southwesterly winds. The division of the whole house into separate units facilitates air flow more than a house built as one single unit.

The group of buildings was located towards the front part of the land and a water-filled ditch was dug at the back so as to provide cool breezes to the house. Like the traditional Thai dwelling, the house was designed to have extended overhangs to shade windows and vents. A trellis shaded the terrace and the deck from sunlight. Fibre glass insulation was

Brick wall next to entrance allowing for cross-ventilation of the interior spaces. Note the carved wooden decorative piece.

placed between two solid walls on the east and west sides which are always exposed to the sun. This was to reduce the amount of heat passing through the walls.

Privacy was achieved by dividing the house into units each of which had been designed according to its function. The house has four main units: a sleeping unit for the parents, another for the children, a

Left: Interior of upstairs living room for family activities.
Left, below: View of an exterior space between adjoining wings. Note construction details, provisions for ventilation and sun protection.

Boonyawat and Pussadee Tiptus are both practising architects in Bangkok, where Mrs. Tiptus is also a teacher at Chulalongkorn Faculty of Architecture. This house, designed for themselves, won a gold medal award in 1984 from the Association of Siamese Architects.

U.S. Ambassador's Residence, Jakarta

Project Data

Location: Taman Suropati, Jakarta.

Client: Embassy of the United States of America, official residence of the Ambassador.

Designer: Interior by Mrs. David Newsom, wife of Ambassador (1974-77); verandah by Mrs. Edward Masters, wife of Ambassador (1977-81).

Interior design: Interior redecorated in 1975, verandah in 1980.

Construction: An art deco-styled Dutch colonial house built in 1928 of reinforced concrete block plastered and painted white, with terracotta tiled roof and large garden.

The Dutch colonial house at Taman Suropati 3, Jakarta, was built in 1928. Because no early documents for the house exist what is known of its history is sketchy, but it has clearly always been considered an important house. Tenants include the managing director of Stanvac Oil Company and the second in command of the Japanese occupation forces during World War II. In 1950 it was purchased by the US Government and has been the official residence of every American Ambassador since Indonesia's independence.

The residence compound has changed over the years. The curved front entrance verandah was glassed in and a new entrance created at the side, giving the house much-needed space to receive guests and hold large official functions. A side verandah was added in 1966 and a swimming pool was built in 1970. During large parties or recep-

Above: An aerial view of the residence compound. The swimming pool was built in 1970.
Below: The residence seen from the wide front garden. The curved entrance verandah was glassed in to provide space to receive guests, who now enter from a portica to the left.

tions guests can now flow from the entrance right through the house to the far verandah.

The interior design has also changed with time as different ambassador's wives have made the house their own. These photographs show the residence as it looked when Ambassador and Mrs. Edward Masters lived there, from 1977 to November 1981.

The dominant colour in the formal reception and dining rooms is blue; all interior walls are white. Furnishings are sparse and understated, giving the rooms a feeling of spaciousness. With the exception of the French furniture in the central hallway and the Hong Kong-made dining room furniture, all the pieces are locally made. The side verandah is furnished in a relaxed and informal style entirely of local materials.

Artwork abounds. Some paintings are on loan from American artists, others are on loan from Indonesian artists or have been purchased for the house. Paintings and artifacts from Thailand, China, Korea and Burma also reflect the Masters' abiding interest in Asian art and culture.

Text by Judith Shaw who works as an editor and lives in Jakarta. Photographs by Christopher Little, a well-known New York photographer who frequently contributes to MIMAR.

Above: The central hallway, with staircase leading to family bedrooms on the second floor. The furniture is French and consists of 19th-Century reproductions of Louis XV pieces. They were left to the house by the first ambassador, Merle Cochrane.
Right: The formal living room with art deco detail on the ventilator over the door. This room is used for small parties and receptions. The abstract painting over the sofa was painted by an American artist, Jane Mahoney and purchased for the house by Mrs. Newsom.

Far left: The dining room is used for formal dinner parties, the largest of which was a sit-down luncheon for thirty-six guests in honour of Vice President Walter Mondale, in May 1978. The room is also used for buffet suppers and cocktail receptions. The batik tablecloth is in the brown parang rusak or "broken knife" motif typical of central Java. The flatware is standard American ambassadorial silver, and the floral arrangements consist of gardenias, frangipani and sprigs of green leaves, all from the residence garden.

Left and left, below: The verandah is the informal heart of the house, and it was here that the Masters spent most of their unofficial time. The space is divided between a sitting area and the family dining area. All the furnishings are local, from the rattan furniture covered with batik, down to the pandanus matting on the floor. Even the lampshades are made with silk from central Java. Indonesian art and handicrafts add accents and personal touches: the carved wooden ducks are from Bali and Lombok, and the large batik painting was commissioned specially for the house from Iwan Tirta, one of Indonesia's best known batik and fashion designers.

The large open area can accommodate many guests when the occasion demands, as in 1981 when seventy-two persons were seated at round tables for a dinner in honour of former President and Mrs. Gerald Ford, in March 1981.

Mr. and Mrs. Masters, former US Ambassador to Indonesia, resident in the house from 1977 to 1981.

William Lim Associates

Goh House, Singapore

Project Data

Location: Emerald Hill
Road, Singapore.
Renovations to two-storey
shophouse.
Floor Area: 338 square
metres.
Renovation Cost: S$200,000
(US$100,000).
Client: Dr. & Mrs. Goh
Poh Seng.
Architects: William Lim
Associates.
Structural, Mechanical &
Electrical Engineers: Steen
Consultants Pte Ltd.
Construction: November
1982 — June 1983.

In August 1981 the Urban Redevelopment Authority (URA) of Singapore announced plans for its first large scale urban conservation project. This proposal for the preservation of about 150 pre-war Malacca style shophouses ensured the preservation of the existing street character as well as the upgrading of the environment through landscaping and the eventual pedestrianisation of Emerald Hill Road. The area was zoned for residential usage with a limited number of commercial shops which had been permitted prior to the exactment of the conservation scheme. Since the announcement, about 15 of the shophouses have undergone renovations.

Dr. Goh and Mrs. Goh had been living in Penang with their family of four sons for a few years and were planning their return to Singapore when they purchased the shophouse at Emerald Hill Road. The building lot has a narrow 5.1 metre frontage and has a depth of approximately 35 metres. The existing structure was in a state of disrepair and had a sagging roof but it was decided that as much of the existing materials and structure as possible would be retained and re-used so that not only the exterior, but the interior character of the house could be preserved. In addition, the Gohs had collected a number of carved timber panels and furniture from old shops and houses in Penang and Singapore which they wanted to incorporate into the new design.

The renovation works turned out to be more extensive than originally envisioned and involved a complete removal of all the existing timber floor joists and timber flooring. The entire roof was removed, new joists and insulation were added and then retiled with the original tiles. A jack roof and skylight were added over the newly created internal courtyard/pool area to introduce light and air into the centre of the house. With the exception of the master bedroom, the house is not airconditioned. The electrical and plumbing works as well as the kitchen installation are all new. Materials for the renovation works were chosen because of their traditional associations and most of the detailing has been interpreted from the traditional shop house. All of the new floors have exposed kapor timber plank flooring and joists. White Carrera marble is used extensively for flooring on the ground level and traditional ceramic ventilation blocks are used both decoratively and for utility.

Below left: Emerald Hill Road elevation. The original facade has been restored with traditional timber windows and ornate plaster work. The double entrance door was acquired from an old house in Penang and reinstalled as part of the renovation works.
Below: Emerald Hill Road. A view along Singapore's first urban conservation project. The Goh's house stands next to a "modernised" version of the shophouse. According to the URA proposal, the facade of such buildings must be restored to approximate the original. Later this year, the street will be paved and landscaped for pedestrians.
Bottom: One of the architect's preliminary sketch models.

**Article by Carl Larson.
Photographs by Andy
Lai and Leong Koh
Loy.**

Above: Detail of the timber panels looking into the dining room. The panels are pivoted so that the space can be opened to include the forecourt and view onto the street.

Left: Carved and gilded timber panels between the entry forecourt and dining room screen the interior of the house from the street.

Above: Furnishings for the living area include some of the Goh's collection of South-East Asian ceramics and sculpture. Beyond is the central courtyard with a 12-foot high palm planted in the centre of the pool.
Right: All of the original exposed timber joists and floors had to be replaced, but the original detailing was retained.

Above and top: The master bedroom looks onto the central court on one side and out over the rear external courtyard on the other. The carved panels framing the wall openings in the master bedroom were originally door frames from an old Penang shophouse.

Left: A view of the central courtyard looking down from the third storey. The height from the pool to the underside of the jack roof is over 11 metres.

Left below: One of the bedrooms on the second level with timber doors and balustrade details derived from the traditional shop house. This room opens out to the courtyard.

Goh Poh Seng is a medical doctor, novelist, playwright and poet. His works deal mainly with South East Asian themes. Currently he is actively involved in a conservation proposal to preserve the Singapore River.

William Lim has his own private practice since 1960. In the design approach to projects, William Lim Associates gives special emphasis to innovative and contextual architecture and environmentally responsive planning.

House Types

TENTS
Lady of the Builders

It seems particularly appropriate for an issue devoted to lightweight structures and nomadic architectures to follow so soon after an issue devoted to the work of women architects in the developing world since, although little acknowledged, it is a fact that the architects of almost all traditionally transient ethnographic societies were, and are, women.[1] Even where tents have evolved into symbols of royalty, into appendages of military strategy and expediency or into the ritual artifact of male-oriented society and behaviour, history suggests a nomadic archetype. Just as social systems never replace others without dramatising the classifications and myths of their predecessors, as if to make permanent their survival on another plane, so the material symbols of passing social systems remain to grant them a last image of themselves.[2]

Until recently, the literature of architectural history tended to exclude the developing areas of the world. It also denied the existence of an architecture of nomadism; hence the role of women in architectural creativity. Monumentality and permanence, traditional tenets of architectural judgement, found few prototypes from the "less civilised" world of ethnographic pastoralists. Anthropology, while attending to those areas within the developing world, has remained the "science of man" in the realm of housing and settlement. Even Amos Rapoport, in his germinal study of house form and culture, makes no mention of the particularly unique phenomenon of gender-related roles in the built environment, and despite our rapidly growing corpus of knowledge about man-environment relationships, the interface between various building activities and gender roles continues to elude us. We suggest that the architecture of nomadism provides an ideal study subject for filling this existing lacuna, and that there are a number of unique but persistent unifying features of nomadic environments which can provide a framework for the pursuit of contemporary concerns.

In the world of nomadism, it has traditionally been the women who have borne the responsibility for creating, erecting, maintaining and demounting the domestic environment, whether it be a tipi, a yurt or a black skin tent. All property relating to it, including the tent and its armature, the furnishings and utensils within it, have come from their hands. Even in those instances where women no longer tan and decorate the vellum or its internal leather furnishings, no longer weave the mats and tapestries themselves, it is still the responsibility of the bride's or wife's family to provide them as part of her dowry or upon the birth of her first child. A woman had ultimate jural rights over her own domain.

In contrast to the ownership of real property, or property with productive potential such as a herd, the ownership of domestic property generates a more intense psychological and poetic expression of identity, involvement and attachment. Emotional masculine involvement with herds, often voiced in pastoral lore, is more than matched by the poetry and metaphor which expresses feminine involvement with her personal domain, her domicile.

The degree to which a place fits our needs and reflects our personality determines our satisfaction with it. We distinguish our personal territory from that of others by "customising" it to suit our individuality, just as we use clothing. Personalised space, so essential to mental health, finds quintessential expression in the traditional mobile structure for several reasons. The investment of individuality in our choice of clothing is most easily extended into the micro environment of a built structure in which the materials of construction of clothing parallel those employed for immediate shelter, whether these be leather, felt or woven goods. We have found the frequent use of matching iconographies worked and woven into the spatial metaphor of both.

In Egypt, the principal deity of architecture and reckoning was the goddess Seshat, "Lady of the builders, of writing and of the House of Books."

In a tent structure, small scale changes are easier to manipulate than large scale changes which require major investment, so that the process of identity is more readily realisable in a kinetic structure. The requisite repetitive assembling and demounting is equivalent to perpetual maintenance which itself intensifies the generation of the creative act. Space is also personalised through continual animated maintenance. Bachelard, quoting Henri Bosco, has called attention to the intense intimacy with our immediate environment generated by the polishing of a tabletop or a candlestick.[3]

---

[1] *The remarks which follow are the coalescence of a long standing interest in women in the architectural profession as a result of personal experience, several decades of research into African architecture and more recent teaching experiences in the studio context. They are also, at the same time, the introduction to some new directions in research which, we hope, may yield new insights into the nature of the design process itself.*
[2] *Jean Duvignaud, The Sociology of Art (New York, 1972), p.9.*
[3] *Gaston Bachelard, The Poetics of Space (Boston, 1969), pp. 68-69.*

Article by Labelle Prussin.
Photographs and drawings courtesy of the author unless otherwise indicated.

Left: An ehen *with its goatskin vellum, from the Hoggar region of southern Algeria.*
Left, below: A matframe ehen *from the Air region of Southern Algeria.*
Photographs: Architecture Slide Library, University of Washington.
Below: Tapestry details and colour preferences found in a wide range of West African tent structures.
Right: A Tuareg ehen *photographed in Haute Volta.*
Right, below: The interior of a Ioullemmeden ehen *with its leather and mat interior, its suspended baggage, calabash supports and tabebut or bed. Photograph: Paul Toucet, Niamey.*

Finally, like other vernacular architectures, there is no distinction or segregation between designer, builder, owner and user: all are one and the same. This homogeneity in the creative process establishes a cosmological, mythological continuum in the built environment which extends from behaviour in space to its ultimate conceptualisation. No other building type embodies such a symbiotic association between occupant and object.

Among the Tuareg people both north and south of the Sahara desert, the *tamakeit* or central pole of the strip-woven or leather vellum tent is conceptually equivalent to the establishment of "place."[1] The term itself derives from the verb *anmenked*, "to support", and is used in both a physical and moral sense. Immediately after it is first erected, Tuareg women, the bearers of the literary traditions, incise or burn apotropaic *tifinar* (the written form of their language) formulas on the *tamakeit* to spiritually guard the interior. Amulets designed to assure the well-being of the tent inhabitants are suspended from

[1] *The Tuareg, often referred to as "the men of the blue veil", are a transhumant population whose territory embraces a vast area of the western Sahara. The population is divided into eight politically and geographically distinct groups, all speaking mutually intelligible dialects of the Berber-derived tamachek language. In spite of their linguistic relationship with Berber, Tuareg life closely approximates that of the Bedouin Arab. However, while other North African nomads have, in general, adopted the animal-hair Black Tent, the Tuareg use a range of skin vellum tents in combination with the Songhay-derived matframe tents. I would like to thank Susanne Curtis for calling my attention to several aspects of Tuareg life which I had been unaware of, during a recent graduate seminar on nomadic architectures.*

this central post, and the same post is used in childbirth. A mother gives birth inside her tent by squatting, bracing herself with the support of the *tamakeit* as she delivers. That this protective and supportive function is extended to include the spiritual realm is evidenced by its frequent appearance in Tuareg poetry as a metaphor for a beneficient force.

The tent itself, called an *ehen*, is synonymous with the Tuareg term for marriage, but it carries a broader meaning than mere abode, since it also implies shelter. One speaks of *ehen n elmusi* as the sheath of a knife, and the term has been extended to mean an entire lineage as well as any kind of house. The women of a household are called *set ehen*, literally "daughters of the tent," and a man proposes to his intended with the words *eg ehen*, literally "mount a tent." Marriage ceremony behaviour itself enacts the symbolic aspects of tent erection and the morning after the "wedding" the marriage tent is taken down and re-erected as a normal tent.

A similar relationship between structure and metaphor can be found in the term *esebar*, which refers to the woven, decorated mats used as side walls. The term derives from the verb *eber*, "to obstruct," and is used in reference to protection from the demons of the void during the period immediately following delivery of a child, when a woman is most vulnerable. The

Above, left: Leatherwork details from saddlebags and cushions made by the Tuareg women leatherworkers in the region of Tahua, Niger. Photograph: Jean Gabus, Musee d'Ethnographie, Neuchatel.
Above: The central support pole or tamakeit used by the Ioullemmeden Tuareg in the region of Niger River Bend, and Tahua, Niger. Photograph: Phototeque Musee de l'Homme.

esebar becomes a spiritually charged boundary, mediating between the sacred and secure interior and the profane, danger-charged exterior.

If we look at the house as symbol of self, then in Tuareg architecture we are looking at the house as symbol of woman. If living space is an extension of the body, and

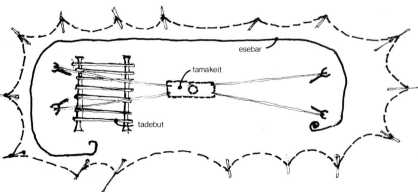

Plan of a vellum tent structure used by the Ioullemmeden Tuareg.

The woven interior of a Djerma (Wogo) nuptial tent using tapestries woven by Fulbe weavers from Niafounke, Mali. Photograph: Paul Toucet, Niamey.

biological as well as social experience influence a woman's preoccupation with the relationship between inside, outside and its mediatory boundaries, then the *ehen* provides, as do other nomadic house forms, an ideal paradigm within which questions regarding distinctive differences between the genders in visuo-spatial aptitudes and in preferences for the quality of space and its pattern gestalts can be considered.

The contrast between male concern with facade and monument and female concern with function and environment, between the male concern with permanence and structural imposition and the female concern with adaptability and psychological need, between the male concern with public image and the female concern with biography and autobiography, is eloquently and poignantly expressed in the environment of tent architectures. The same polarities find expression in the nature of the Tuareg design process itself, in which the preference for cumulative building element assemblage from associated fragments from the inside out, constrasts sharply with the fixed view from the outside in, which is so characteristic of creativity in the monumental tradition. The Tuareg bed or *tadebut,* itself an assemblage of demountable elements, also serves as the measure of interior space and is used to establish the boundary of the matframe tents which some southern Tuareg clans use.

It has been suggested that the precise cardinal orientation of nomadic structures and their rigid division of interior space is a response to the deep psychological need for the sense of security which comes from knowing where one is, socially as well as territorially.[1] The more featureless the context of actual territorial space, the more rigid and artificial the model must be. It is no accident that the conical *tipi,* the domical *yurt* or the beehive matframe *ehen* are a response to the expanse of the North American plains, the windblown steppes of Mongolia and the sandblown savannah-sahel of North and West Africa. One is tempted to recall Bachelard's discussion of roundness and his suggestion that when a thing becomes isolated, it becomes round, assuming a figure of being concentrated upon itself.[2]

At the same time, a house constitutes a body of images that give humanity the proof or illusion of stability. A house is a place in which a human being's certainty of being is concentrated. And yet, a transient structure, perpetually moving along albeit familiar lines, is the antinomy of stability. Nomads, semi-nomads and transhumants, whose life consists of continuous, seasonal

[1]Edmund Leach, Culture and Communication (Cambridge, 1976), pp. 53-54.
[2]Bachelard, op. cit. pp. 232ff.

displacement necessitated by the search for and acquisition of subsistence, find themselves confronted with an apparent paradox: the need for stability affording shelter and protection and the need for mobility affording sustenance. The resolution of the contradiction is in a response which creates a closed miniature world in the form of cone, cube or dome whose interior manifests an intense emphasis on richness of surface and colour. Bare and unadorned exterior surfaces are matched by elaborate interior detail, abundant with metaphor and iconography.

The sense of hiding and secrecy which such enclosure affords is reflected in the Fulbe *bororo* (nomadic) concept of space. Within the feminine hemisphere of the *wuro* or encampment, one finds one or more *suudu* or house units in the form of a basketlike, matframe tent. The term *suudu* derives from the verb "to hide," and it is a place where a being or thing finds shelter. The term carries with it the notion of compartment and a sense of hiding. Thus, the same term, like the Tuareg *ehen,* can be used in reference to a place where a person sleeps, to the envelope of a letter, a box, or a case in which objects are stored.

In contrast to the carpentered environ-

Left: Fulbe suudu *on the outskirts of Goundham, Mali.*

Left, below: Fulbe bororo *women erecting a* suudu *or matframe tent in Mali.*

Photograph: Marli Shamir.

ments of sedentary lifestyles and high tech societies, nomadic environments are soft and malleable, derivative of minimally modified natural materials. Materials of construction, materials used in the demarcation of assigned spaces and the mechanisms for privacy are evocative of early tactile experience associated with well-being.

It has been well documented that with the onset of sedentarisation, sex-role changes occur at all levels of social organisation. Shifts in power structures are reflected in property resources and in changes associated with building tasks and responsibilities per se. These can all be indexed by eventual changes in the built form, in the content of behaviours relative to the location and position of structural elements, and in the organisation, content and figural quality of decorative elements associated with the built form.[1]

Paradoxically, trends in contemporary society include increasing personal and social mobility, fragmentation and alienation from the natural environment, as well as further shifts in gender roles and rights. Current trends appear to be re-creating, at a higher level, many of the characteristic features of traditional nomadic societies. The in-depth study of their architecture of portable roots can, we believe, reveal some innovative insights and more appropriate design directions withhin a world of high technology, geometrically ordered living environments with their impersonal, bleak and barren surfaces.

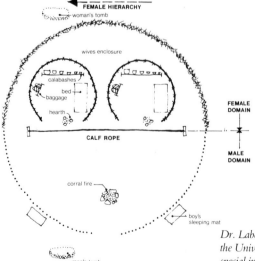

FEMALE HIERARCHY

woman's tomb

wives enclosure

calabashes

bed

baggage

hearth

CALF ROPE

FEMALE DOMAIN

MALE DOMAIN

corral fire

boy's sleeping mat

man's tomb

MALE HIERARCHY

Plan of a Fulbe bororo encampment.

[1] *See Labelle Prussin, "Fulani-Hausa Architecture: Genesis of a Style," in African Arts 9,3 (1976) for a discussion and examples of this phenomenon among the Fulbe-speaking peoples in West Africa.*

Dr. Labelle Prussin is Professor of Architecture at the University of New York, New York and has a special interest in peripheral communities of the developing world. She has written numerous books and articles and is the author of a recent book entitled 'Hatumere. Islamic Design in West Africa'

Houses of Upper Volta

by Jean-Paul Bourdier

*Jean-Paul Bourdier has prepared especially for MIMAR
a study of Gurunsi houses in Upper Volta.
The author completed the original study three years ago
in collaboration with students from the School of Architecture of Dakar, Senegal.
It was aimed at discovering for architects in West Africa
alternative sources of inspiration to the Greek Order values
taught by Beaux Arts-educated teachers.*

*Bourdier, a Frenchman, left Senegal
and is now teaching at the Department of Architecture
at the University of California, Berkeley.*

*The text, photographs and drawings presented here
are excerpted from the study by Jean-Paul Bourdier
with Nddngo Athj, Innocent Bimenyimana, Trinh Thi Minh-Ha Bourdier,
Makhtar Faye, El Hadj Malik Gaye, Sharon Murray,
Mame Didulame Seye and N dary Toure.*

*Photograph above: Exterior decoration
on a Kussace house in Yuga.*

In a time when we realise the significance of a subsistence economy it is important to understand the technological and sociological value of vernacular architecture — an architecture by people, done without commercial considerations. This new sympathy does not imply that we should currently imitate it, but to consider it for a constant questioning and refining of solutions for present architectural projects.

A number of problems generated by industrial production in Western societies are reflected in many "modern" housing schemes. The absence of territoriality and natural surveillance, the lack of transition from public

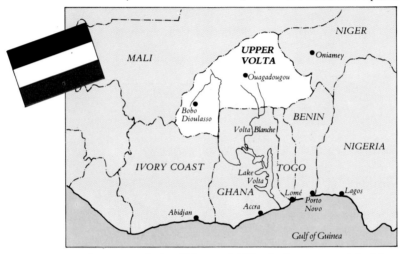

Republic of Upper Volta

Area: 274,200 square kilometres (105,869 square miles)
Population: 6,815,000
Capital: Ouagadougou; population 173,000
History: Descendants of Mossi warriors, who rejected conversion to Islam in the 11th century, make up half the population today. Population pressures on the drought-prone savannas of the Sahel, drive farmers into neighbouring countries as seasonal labour. Landlocked Upper Voltans depend on a railroad lifeline to the Ivory Coast. Independence from France came in 1960. A military government stepped aside in 1978 in favour of civilian rule.
Religions: Traditional, Muslim, Christian.
Languages: French, Mossi, Lobi, Samo, Gourounsi.
Literacy: 10%.
Life expectancy: 42 years.
Economy: Industries — food processing, textiles. Export crops — cotton, shea nuts, livestock. Domestic consumption — sorghum, millet, corn.
Per capita income: US$180.

to private space, the insufficiency of children's play space, and the failure to integrate old people into everyday activities are among the environmental/sociological problems. Identical processes are observable in African urban areas and in an ever-growing number of rural settlements.

Low-rise buildings within high-density developments, interior private courtyards, self-help building, expandable units, and passive energy systems are concepts now studied and praised in the West which have been used for centuries in African, Middle Eastern and Southeast Asian architectures. But few of these studies in architectural anthropology have been used to improve new African towns or rural settlements. What other than military and sanitary concerns can we trace in the French colonial planning of towns in Senegal, Mali or Upper Volta? In what way is the present use of square-grid planning, wide streets for cars, and high or middle-rise housing adapted to African patterns of living?

The condescension implied by such a word as "primitive" architecture — associated with the idea that sophistication and complexity is progress — has contributed to the lack of confidence, by many ethnic groups, in their own cultural background. As a consequence, similar to buying outdated surplus goods from the West, many African cultures are adopting the same patterns of living that the West is now finding unsuitable for itself. Aside from the long-term material drawbacks, the social and psychological side effects are bound to be at least as great as in the West since the gap between tradition and modernism is larger in Africa, and the time for adaptation to change much shorter.

Traditionally the sub-Saharan adobe house is built and maintained by the whole family during the dry season when no farming takes place. With the import of new ideas, such as having specialised labour to build a house with "modern" materials like concrete blocks and zinc sheet roofing, vernacular architecture is disappearing at an alarming speed. Very few of the houses presented here are still standing.

Kassena dwellings at Tangassoko

Top: A typical decorated house. This structure in a larger compound is the man's unit. Note the low entrance and the ladder to the right which gives access to the roof terrace.
Above: Men's quarters. The exterior of the men's units are more elaborately decorated than the women's. The black colour infill in the patterns is of asphalt which replaces the old traditional grey-black colour obtained from ground stone.

In order to avoid an analysis centred on Western values, we tried in our survey to retrieve the significance and root of local words used to designate an object or a space. We noticed that a number of terms such as "head" or "mouth of the house" denoted anthropomorphic symbolism; none of these terms, however, ever referred to a specific function such as cooking, eating or sleeping. In observing the various ethnic groups which constitute the Gurunsi people, we found that the main space in the house is multi-functional. It is used for sleeping, storing goods, eating, meeting friends, spinning cloth, weaving baskets, and as play-space for children. On the other hand, during certain months of the dry season, the adjacent courtyard is used for the same activities. Any family member can use these two spaces at any time of the day or night: this creates a web of visual, auditory and tactile relationships which can hardly be described by definite functional words as the ones used above. It is probably to such a variety of visible and non-visible links that people refer when they use the term "organic" architecture.

The labelling of each family's genealogical tree directly onto the plans we drew was also an attempt to not reduce definition of spaces to mere function but to relate them to the building's evolution, the densities of occupation and the development of the family structure.

The study of this foreign culture kept our minds alert to the subtlety of codes we had to decipher in order to avoid misinterpreting the local flow of life. It allowed us to observe and question our ingrained concepts with renewed eyes. For example, the observation of a Kassena tribe member's house raised several points, such as the reasons for its low and rather torturous entrance: Why such an entry? Once inside the house one could also wonder why there is such a low intensity of light, or why the tactile seems emphasised over the visual. Trying to understand even one element of that environment is like trying to comprehend a person: it leads to the realisation that everything is inter-related and the exploration and questioning is a never ending chain.

In the vernacular architecture of Upper Volta careful attention is given to details and transitions, since man is the measure of the surroundings. Questioning each element of this architecture can reveal the accumulated experience and wisdom of several generations: it challenges our habits of solving building problems and widens our architectural framework of reference.

Section of a Kassena compound in Tangassoko. The main space on the right depicts the 'mouth' entrance where one has to stoop down, then stand halfway up and finally stride over a low wall before gaining access to the room. Some of the functions of this entrance are protection against rain, wind and animals. As it is hard to get in or out quickly, the entry deters thieves or enemies and allows the occupant inside to fire an arrow at the intruder's leg, while the latter cannot do the same.

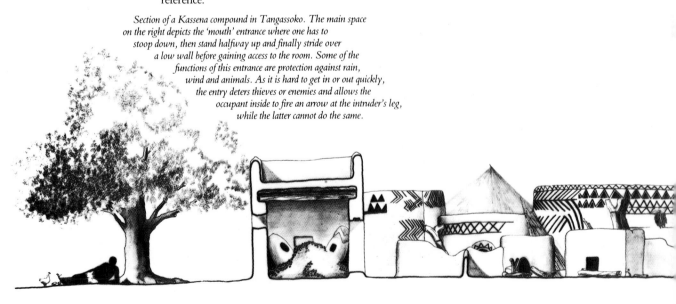

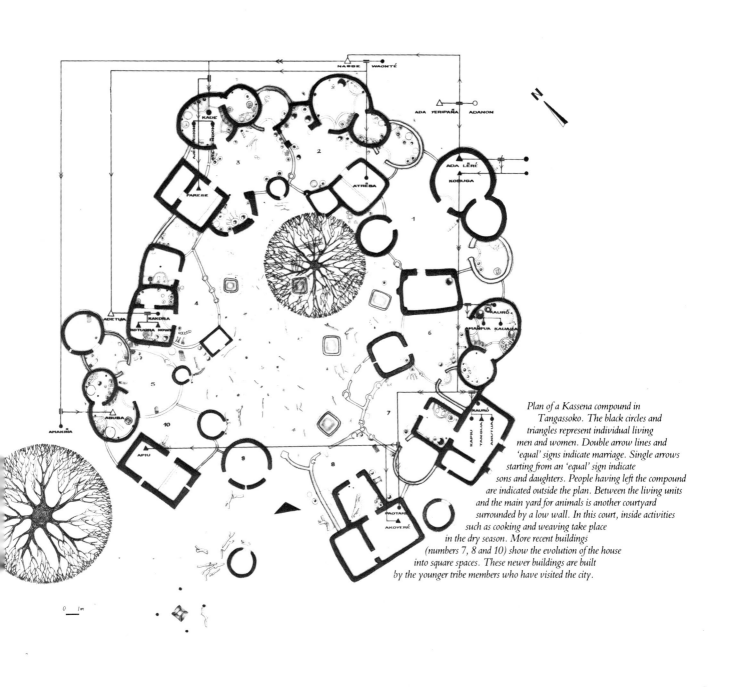

Plan of a Kassena compound in Tangassoko. The black circles and triangles represent individual living men and women. Double arrow lines and 'equal' signs indicate marriage. Single arrows starting from an 'equal' sign indicate sons and daughters. People having left the compound are indicated outside the plan. Between the living units and the main yard for animals is another courtyard surrounded by a low wall. In this court, inside activities such as cooking and weaving take place in the dry season. More recent buildings (numbers 7, 8 and 10) show the evolution of the house into square spaces. These newer buildings are built by the younger tribe members who have visited the city.

0   1m

0   1m

Nankana dwellings at Yuka

Above: Elevation. The small, round openings have appeared in the past few decades since cessation of tribal rivalries.
Left: Cutaway of a woman's dwelling space. Several of these units are located in a circle around a courtyard. Animals are not allowed into the open tamped court (zinzaka).
The cooking area (saraga) used in the rainy season moves to the danga, *covered with millet stems, in the dry season or eventually to the gongonga for important gatherings on special occasions.*
The stairs expand to the roof, the area for sleeping or drying grains. During the day the temperature can reach 48°C but the inside temperature is about 8°C lower.

Left: House. The horizontal adobe strip reinforces the wall and prevents vertical cracking from settlements.
Above: The large staircase to the roof at the house allows easy access and carrying of goods. The low entrance is typical of Upper Voltan vernacular architecture.

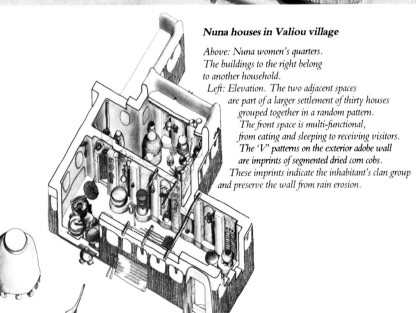

Nuna houses in Valiou village

Above: Nuna women's quarters.
The buildings to the right belong
to another household.
 Left: Elevation. The two adjacent spaces
    are part of a larger settlement of thirty houses
        grouped together in a random pattern.
        The front space is multi-functional,
        from eating and sleeping to receiving visitors.
        The 'V' patterns on the exterior adobe wall
        are imprints of segmented dried corn cobs.
    These imprints indicate the inhabitant's clan group
and preserve the wall from rain erosion.

0   1m

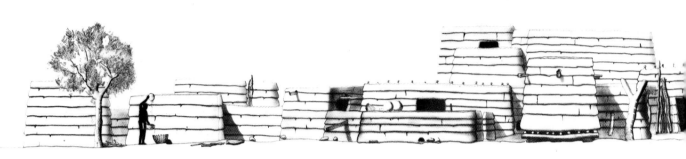

Pougouli house at Niemo

Above: Front elevation. The wall is built of
layers of adobe rammed on top of each other.
Left: Cutaway of a house, belonging to an
extended family. A single entrance gives access to
a long corridor in which goats are kept at night.
Openings on either side of the corridor
lead to single family living units.
The post and beam structure allows the walls
to meander, and creates a number of smaller spaces.
When these smaller spaces are not enclosed,
they allow the main central area (Zaré) to expand.
The walled court of each unit — at the lower
and upper parts of the drawing —
can only be reached through each Zaré.

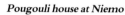

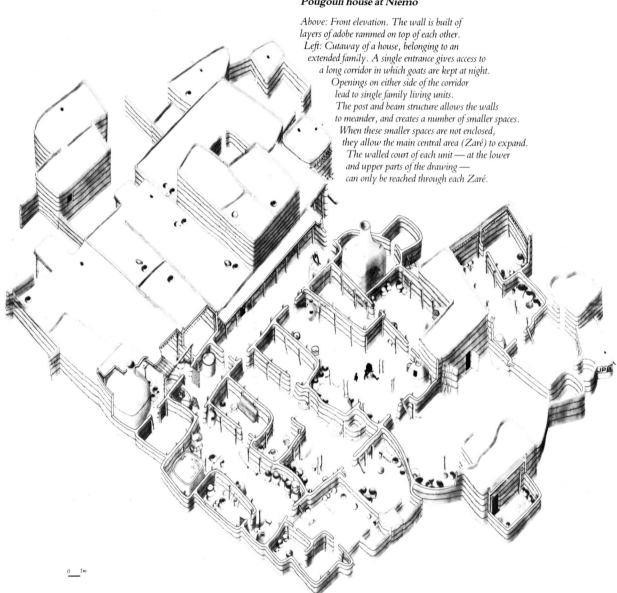

0   1m

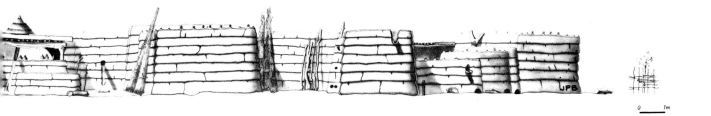

0   1m

*Left: A grain silo at Niemo. The grain is poured into
it from the top.*
Above: House.

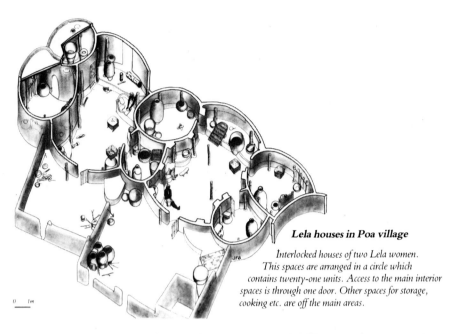

Lela houses in Poa village

*Interlocked houses of two Lela women.
This spaces are arranged in a circle which
contains twenty-one units. Access to the main interior
spaces is through one door. Other spaces for storage,
cooking etc. are off the main areas.*

0   1m

*Above: The exterior elevation of a compound. The
white areas are painted with ash. They indicate the
owner's clan, reflect the hot sun's rays and serve as an
insect repellent.*
*Left: The interior of the main space of a Lela woman's
quarters. The floor is always below the natural ground
level — the excavated earth is tamped onto the roof.
Ledges of earth are left along the walls to provide sitting
and storage areas.*

Traditional Kuwaiti Houses

This is the first of a two-part photo-essay on the domestic architecture of Kuwait. The author presents a few traditional houses in this article, and in the second will look at contemporary dwellings.
Text and photographs by **Huda Al-Bahar**.

The rapid urban growth of Kuwait City over the last thirty years has been almost unparalleled in the history of urbanism. And the city's "building boom," richly nourished by the country's oil revenues, has had dramatic effects on the existing historic urban fabric. The speedy architectural and urban developments have indiscriminately disintegrated the anatomy and identity of the traditional city, eliminating most of its charming traditional architecture. Today, only a handful of the older Kuwaiti buildings remain intact, most of which are dwellings. Some of those have recently been renovated and are being used at present as museums housing various exhibits for the general public.

The examples portrayed here do not represent the prevalent residential architecture of the traditional city, as only the houses of the more affluent residents have managed to survive the destructive forces of the rapid urban development. Nevertheless, the prevailing design concepts and architectural character inherent in many of the traditional dwellings can be clearly identified and represented by the illustrated examples.

The charm and beauty of Kuwait's traditional architecture (dating between the latter part of the 18th century to the first half of the 20th century) lay in its simple, functional and rational approach to vernacular design.

A comfortable living environment that responded to human, social, cultural and environmental needs was the dominant concept, and it defined the main character of the traditional dwellings.

Among the many design features of the older houses of Kuwait was the cultural concept of separating male and female quarters and the notion of privacy and security. Consequently, the plan of most of those residences consisted of separate men's and women's quarters. The men's rooms usually faced or fronted the street and occasionally had

windows, while the women's quarters were set back and secluded, having no windows facing the street, except occasionally on a second level when wooden grilles or shutters were used on the windows to provide privacy. Quite often the female quarters had access to a back street through a side doorway while the main entrance to the house led to the men's quarters.

The courtyard was another important element that played a vital social and environmental role. Socially, the courtyard

Left: The Sheikh's palace on Failaka Island, Kuwait. The palace has been renovated, and functions at present as the Failaka museum. The building is sited on slightly elevated ground, in a rather secluded setting, independent of other buildings, and hence no provisions were made for open courtyards in the interior. Outdoor activities could be carried outside, and privacy could be ensured, due to the isolated nature of the location. Doors and windows were utilised on almost all facades of the building to ensure cross-ventilation.
Left, below: The remaining old part of Al-Zour Village (Failaka Island, Kuwait) partially portrays the urban character of the older city of Kuwait, no longer in existence due to the unprecedented, rapid urban development that the city has undergone over the last 30 years. The organic urban matrix composed of narrow streets flanked by walls of mud buildings and vertically accentuated by the many minaret silhouettes represents the urban setting for many of the traditional dwellings of Kuwait.

functioned as a dynamic space where people gathered to socialise in an open, yet private living setting, and environmentally, it effectively modified climatic conditions. The courtyard permitted outdoor activities while providing a significant level of protection from the wind, dust, sand, solar glare, and heat characteristic of Kuwait's climate. The surrounding loggia, arcaded at times, prevented direct sunlight from entering interior spaces and hence assisted in the control and reduction of heat gain in the buildings. In the more affluent homes, a number of courtyards were utilised for various social functions.

The roof had always been an extensively used part of the

house. In the hot summer months, it provided a cool and breezy space for people to sleep. Other activities, such as bathing, washing clothes and drying fruit were also carried out on the roof. Slightly sloping to the exterior, the roof structure incorporated wooden water-spouts which, quite often, had decorative wooden lips to regulate the water flow. Many of the more affluent residences had roofs with ornamented parapet walls which provides the desired level of privacy while allowing a view of the outside.

A very important element in the design of the larger residences was the presence of the *diwan*, a public gathering and entertainment place for men. It was often located close to the main entrance of the house, fronting the street. Sometimes windows facing the street were used and those were protected with bars, wooden grilles and/or shutters.

The kitchen was located in the women's quarters and hence it had no windows to the outside. The food was prepared in pots, heated on masonry stoves. Water for drinking and cooking was often brought in by tanker from Basra and stored in large pots due to the scarcity of fresh water at that time. Brackish water known as *sulaibiya* was used for washing and it was frequently stored in roof top tanks. A few houses had a built well, locally known as a *jeleeb*, placed in the centre of the courtyard to collect rainwater.

The house was constructed of indigenous materials. Sun-dried mud pellets or seashore rocks were mortared with mud to form the walls which were finally faced with mud plaster. The thickness of the walls provided the insulation required to modify the rather harsh climate in the hot summer months. The roof was supported on round wooden poles, known locally as *chandles*. Reed mats, holding mud mixed with straw, were placed on top

of the wooden poles to form the ceilings of the rooms and the roof floor. A second storey, primarily a wooden structure, was added to provide more living space in some of the larger dwellings.

The modest yet distinguished ornamentation used to embellish and accent certain building events was no less charming than the ingenious architectural manipulation of form and space in response to the many living needs of the community. It is here that one can quote Voltaire: "When one has completed the necessary ... One immediately comes upon the beautiful and the pleasing." And it is in the humble and unpretentious architectural ornament, the beautiful and the pleasing, that the enrichment of

architectural knowledge beyond the necessities of survival was clearly perceived by the early builders of Kuwait. An architectural knowledge sought a fulfillment of a spiritual need for a celebration of what was considered to be an important architectural experience.

The many decorative motifs were often inspired by eastern influences, mostly Persian, Iraqi and Indian in origin. This was not surprising, as the Kuwaiti merchants at that time travelled extensively to the East for trade and other commercial activities.

Among the many decorative features of the traditional Kuwaiti dwellings, the distinctive Kuwaiti doors were perhaps the finest and the most prominent. They were constructed of teak, mostly imported from Africa. Horizontal crossbars held together the vertical planks, and dome-shaped nails were used as fasteners. Each door was embellished with carved floral patterns, usually on the cover-piece between the two doors. The door frames were often left plain with occasional

Kuwaiti doors are a very distinctive element of a house. This entrance door is made up of flat vertical slats of wood bound together by cross pieces and metalwork. The dome-shaped nails and ironwork door knockers are both decorative and integral to the construction.

simple mouldings. A *bejurer* or a smaller inset door was frequently constructed within the large pair of doors, using similar crossbars and vertical planks. The predominant use of bosses and rosettes in the carving on many of such doors had been clearly an inspiration by early Persian and Iraqi (Mesopotamian) art.

Other decorative features were celebrated in the arcaded loggia of some of the courtyards. Here stucco ornament, curvilinear, geometric or floral in nature was employed to embellish the arcades and other spaces surrounding the courtyard. Carved column capitals were also utilised in a few of the courtyards to emphasise and celebrate the enclosing colonnade.

As mentioned earlier, the roof parapets of many of the buildings exhibited a variety of geometric and floral decorative motifs, manipulated in a manner that allowed the passage of breezes for roof ventilation while maintaining the desired level of privacy for the occupants.

The windows often incorporated wooden shutters to reduce and control heat gain and glare. Wooden or iron bars were often constructed on the exterior for security. In most cases, the fenestration ornament was absent or kept to a minimum in the traditional dwellings.

The distinctive character of the traditional residential architecture of Kuwait had been manifested in its rational and pragmatic approach to creating an optimum living environment for life as it was then. The concepts and methods utilised by the early builders possessed a level of sensitivity and intuition strongly delineated by an overriding human dimension, a dimension that identified the modest yet distinguished personality of the traditional Kuwaiti dwellings.

Sadu house (formerly the Behbehani house).

The building has been renovated and is used at present as a museum exhibiting locally made Bedouin rugs (sadu). The front facade, facing the sea, employs two well-defined entrances into the building. The overall architectural composition is rather unusual in a number of ways, including the platforming of the overall building structure, the generous use of fenestration at both levels, and the decorative motifs employed to embellish and accentuate the various architectural events. Much of the building ornament has been inspired by Indian influences, and this is perhaps best seen in the use of the pointed Mogul arch of the recessed building entrance to the left.

Right: Interior courtyard showing the rather unusual colonnade leading into the interior spaces. The heavy masonry columns are anchored on rectangular bases ornamented with an abstract floral motif, coloured in brown and executed in relief. The top of the columns and the capitals display very modest stucco carving, also utilising a floral motif. The roof parapet is very finely executed, integrating ornament with a perforated lattice-like network to allow for the passage of breezes.

Below: The main entrance into the reception court. The decorative motifs of the Mogul arch and the very finely executed floral mouldings and carvings on the panels of the recessed door have been clearly inspired by Indian work.

Below, right: Detail of ornament on the door. Intricately executed floral motifs embellish the door panels, the door frame, and the cover-piece between the two doors.

Below: Window detail, showing the use of the pointed-arch frame to define the fenestration. A finely executed metal lattice or grille is used on the exterior for security, while wooden shutters are used for the control of ventilation and light.

133

Al-Ghanim house, main entrance. This building has been renovated and is currently occupied by artists. The courtyards and other interior spaces are used at present as working spaces for the artists as well as spaces for public art exhibits. The entrance doors are characteristic of the traditional architecture, although the bejurer or smaller inset door is absent.

Key

1. Entrance Passage
2. Men's Reception Court
3. Loggia
4. Men's Reception Room (diwan)
5. Bathroom
6. Kitchen
7. Animal Court
8. Private Living Court
9. Family Living Room
10. Women's Reception Room
11. Sleeping Room
12. Business Court
13. Well
14. Kitchen Court
15. Storeroom
16. Small Yard
17. Masonry Bench
18. Coffee Room

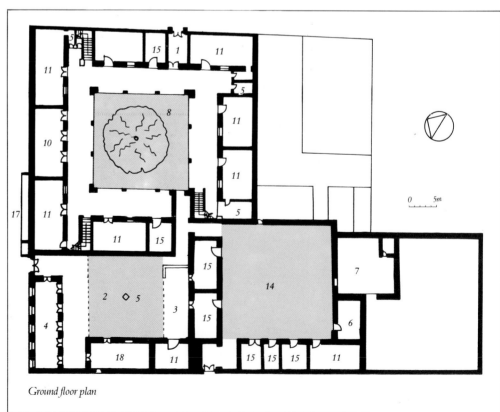

Ground floor plan

Left: Detail of the doors of the main entrance, showing the dome-shaped nails commonly used as fasteners, and the decoration utilised on the cover strip between the two doors, comprised mostly of clusters of bosses.
Above and right: The interior square-tiled courtyard, showing (to the left) the men's reception hall, the doors of which exhibit Turkish decorative motifs and incorporate semi-circular fanlights. The main entrance to the building is seen on the right at the end of the short passageway. The columns utilised to support the roof are polygonal in plan, and exhibit rather intricate woodcarving decoration to celebrate the capitals. The wooden water spouts of the roof are seen projecting horizontally.

135

Al-Bader house

The building has been renovated, and is currently used as the Kuwait National Museum. The front facade, facing the sea, shows the main entrance to the building, with the characteristic Kuwaiti doors, set back in an arched and vaulted entry space. The exterior of the building is to a large extent left plain, and the wooden water-spouts are clearly seen projecting horizontally from the roof.

Above: The men's reception court, showing the arcaded loggia. Piers of an octagonal shape widen at the top to meet the four pointed corners of the square capitals decorated with a scalloped motif. The pointed arches, supported by the piers, are also framed in a scalloped decorative manner. The men's reception hall can be seen beyond the arcaded loggia.

Right: The men's reception room or diwan. The wall ornament is comprised of a repetitive pattern of rectangular niches, bordered by a painted decoration in low relief. The decorative motif represents a floral pattern flanking the sides of a plain panel. The vertical ornament is painted dark-blue, and the horizontal is orange. (Above these niches is the stucco ornament described in the photograph far right, above).

Al-Bader house

136

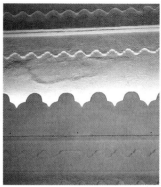

Left: Arcaded loggia outside the men's reception room, leading into the reception court. The piers supporting the pointed arches are octagonal. They widen at the top to meet the four pointed corners of the square capitals decorated with a scalloped motif. The ornament on the exterior wall of the men's reception room is comprised of waist-high niches. A dark-blue decoration panel in relief lies to the sides of these niches, and above, horizontal bands of a scalloped motif painted gold and blue are topped by plain niches of projecting scalloped decoration that finally meet the characteristic ceiling of the Kuwaiti traditional architecture.
Above: Stucco ornament in the men's reception room. The whitewashed wall is ornamented with horizontal bands of a scalloped decorative motif. The bands are stepped in projection from the face of the wall. An inverted scalloped motif in the form of a pelmet has been added recently to camouflage the electric lighting used in the display spaces of the museum.
Left: The private living court was used by the family. Surrounding it is the family living room and the sleeping rooms.

Key
1. Entrance passage
2. Men's reception court
3. Loggia
4. Men's reception room (diwan)
5. Bathroom
6. Kitchen
7. Animal court
8. Private living court
9. Family living room
10. Women's reception room
11. Sleeping room
12. Business court
13. Well
14. Kitchen court
15. Storeroom
16. Small yard
17. Masonry bench
18. Coffee room
19. Animal stalls
20. Business office

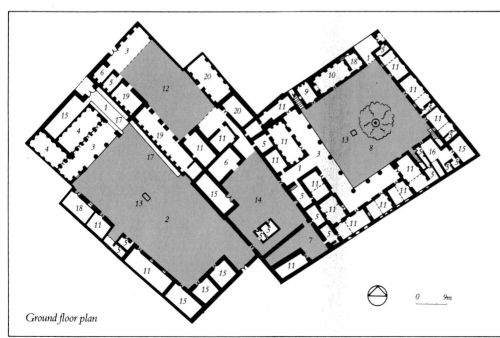

Ground floor plan

0   9m

Left: The passageway between the private living court and the kitchen court, showing the piers and pointed arches of the arcaded loggia of the private living court.
Below: The kitchen, showing the bread oven raised on a platform with a hole in the centre. The food is prepared in pots heated by masonry over an open fire.
Bottom: The coffee room, showing the sunken rectangular hearth on the floor where coffee is prepared over charcoal. A raised masonry bench behind the hearth is used to store the brass coffee jugs. Locally made wool rugs and cushions are often utilised to furnish the interior in the winter, while straw or reed mats are used in the summer.

Contemporary Kuwaiti Houses

This is the second and concluding part of a photo-essay on the domestic architecture of Kuwait — part one was featured in MIMAR 13.
Text and photographs by Huda Al-Bahar unless otherwise indicated.

The changes in architecture experienced by Kuwait over the last thirty years or so, are almost beyond imagination. The tremendous visual impact that recent structures have had and still continue to have on the built environment can only be accurately described by actual experience. The feeling might perhaps be comparable to visiting a Disneyland of residential manifestations!

Having generally examined the character of the traditional dwellings (in MIMAR 13), I felt it would be interesting to investigate the multitude of modern residential architecture in the context of what is known about the traditional examples already presented. I therefore will attempt to provide as realistic a picture as possible of the changes and transformations that have led to the birth of a hodgepodge of architectural forms.

This article only investigates the private villas in Kuwait and does not incorporate any form of government housing. It is also worth noting that due to the diversity of the houses featured, the nature of the text is quite general. The main objective is to present the eclectic character of the residential environment in Kuwait, best expressed by the dressed up exteriors of the buildings. Consequently, the examination of specific buildings is not necessary for the purpose of this article. Finally, I present some personal views on architectural aesthetics and evaluation in the context of the residential manifestations that have surfaced in Kuwait.

Early Post Oil period 1950's — early 1960's

Left: An example of Kuwait's residential architecture of the 1950's and early 1960's. The geometric nature of the facade is expressed by the angled concrete slabs, punched with various openings for purely decorative purposes. The multi-colour scheme of the plastered exterior, the zig-zagged roof canopy, the large balconies supported by the rather unusual columns, the waffled balcony ceilings and the iron doors of the main entrance, set in a geometric form and topped with a jetlike canopy are all characteristic architectural features of this period.

Left, below: Another example of Kuwait's Early Post Oil residential architecture. The distinctive architectural features of this period are well expressed by the geometric and technicolour plastered facade, the sloping zig-zagged roof canopy, the angled and punched decorative concrete slabs, the large balconies with their multi-colour hollow waffled ceilings and the very characteristic main entrance set in a geometric concrete form, angled at the sides and topped with a canopy. Photographs: T. Allison.

Many of the vast urban and architectural changes that have taken place in Kuwait over the last thirty years have been a direct result of a capital-surplus oil-fed economy. The traditional city was demolished in order to give way to modern infrastructure. As a result, the residents of the old town had to be re-located in newly planned neighbourhood units that Kuwait's Post Oil Era eclectic architecture has been so overwhelmingly expressed.

The overall affluence allowed the increased acquisition of motor cars, the introduction of new technologies, the importation of architects, engineers, other professionals and labourers from various parts of the world, in an effort to build the modern Kuwait. The newcomers, many of whom were Arabs, did not quite understand the various aspects of Kuwait's environment. The Kuwaiti citizen himself did not quite comprehend what architecture was all about. The Kuwaitis began to experience a sense of freedom from the constraints of the traditional way of life and a sense of affluence toward a modern living environment. They began with the aid of rather mediocre architects to express their confused thoughts architecturally. Many of their attempts were in search of a new identity that had no link with the past, and rather than develop, enhance and refine the traditional character in the context of the new, they simply discarded the old and started to build the new on very shaky and superficial grounds. And it is this disruption in the process of environmental change that has resulted in the failure of most of what I call Kuwait's Early Post Oil architecture in

Early Post Oil period

Left: This renovated example with multi-coloured plastered exterior has been re-painted white. Some of the balconies have been closed in and the main entrance has been replaced with rather modest aluminium doors. Many of the other features of the original design are however still apparent. They include the large picture windows, the spacious balconies that have not been closed in, the sloping roofs and roof canopies and the angled elevations punched with openings at times.

the 1950's.

This period can generally be characterised by its residential designs that express quite astonishing gestures in the name of modernism. The geometry plays a dominant role as a facade element giving the building an image of a jigsaw puzzle, a cardboard model but not a residence as conceived by

Mouhammed Al-Hamad's Residence

Above: A product of the late 1960's. Disenchanted with the technicolour geometric manifestations of the Early Post Oil period, this example utilises brick, in a simple pattern, as a more durable veneer material. Fenestration and balconies are reduced and the windows are set back to provide some protection from the sun.

Right: The main stairway, to the left of the entrance hall. The finest craftsmanship of wood and stained glass are exquisitely executed. The intricate

geometric and floral motifs along with the panels of Quranic inscriptions are all hand carved and painted.

Far right: The main hall. The ceilings, walls, doors and furniture are all hand carved and painted in floral and geometric motifs. The workmanship is mainly of Syrian origin. The final decorative touches which include the ornate chandelier, lanterns and side lamps, the silver vases, the wooden chest, the fine Persian carpet and the brass door handles are all carefully selected to complement the finishes and furniture.

most people. Sloping roof canopies at acute, oblique, skew or deformed angles, unfunctional decorative slabs of concrete punched with various openings, aided by a technicolour elevation loudly reject any association with the past. Jet-like structures and flying rockets became a symbol of modern living.

The failure of this period of Kuwait's architecture was felt even more in the poor performance of the building itself in terms of providing a comfortable living environment. Air-conditioning technology allowed large picture windows and spacious balconies to be used. This caused tremendous maintenance and environmental comfort problems, due to the severe hot climate, accompanied by dust in the blistering summer months. The stuccoed or plastered multicolour exteriors peeled and weathered very poorly, and along with the balconies that were later closed in for lack of use, resulted in unsightly elevations.

Fortunately, the offensive residential architecture of that period did not remain popular for very long. People became aware of the problems that such designs entailed and this allowed them to seek more modest and functional structures although the question of aesthetics was still to be resolved.

But alas the awareness did not last too long. The country and citizens witnessed even greater affluence in the 1970's. The wealth allowed many people to travel extensively around the world, bringing home images of their future dream houses. The individualistic statement of each residential form became of paramount importance in the Middle Post Oil period of Kuwait's architecture. People perceived their house as a symbol of their affluence and status in society and each individual was compelled to state uniqueness in architecture. This in turn generated the eclectic forms that are so much part of the Kuwaiti residential architectural scene today. Neo-classical, Baroque, Neo-Islamic, Bungalow style, Spanish, North African, Cubist, Neo-Bedouin, outer space you name it, you'll find it … and even more!

Some of the private villas of this period are quite handsome structures and could be quite appealing if sited on acres of greenland, standing as individual buildings, amidst luscious landscapes and running water. But unfortunately the eclectic dwellings stand side by side in Kuwait's residential neighbourhoods to display an architectural extravaganza, a carnival, a showroom of copied styles and motifs, results of confused aesthetic values and a lack of understanding of a need to develop one's own architectural identity. Perhaps the only positive things I can say about much of this period's architecture is that more durable materials have been utilised on the exterior (mostly veneer masonry), balconies have been reduced, if not eliminated, and attempts have

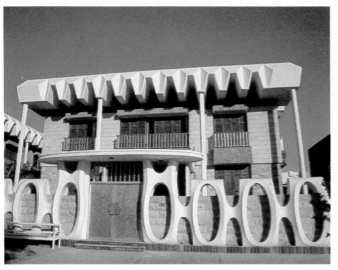

Middle Post Oil period
Mid 1960's-1970's

Left: As manifestation that attempts to produce an individualistic architectural statement. The confused and irrational facade treatment adds yet another cosmetic design approach to Kuwait's eclectic architectural scene.

Below: An eclectic example of this period. A monumental, pseudo plazzo image is strongly portrayed through the use of the rather large, but flat central dome, the arched windows, the balconies and the multitude of facade materials utilised (limestone, sandstone, travertine, marble, tile, plaster etc.). The inconsistency in the exterior elements are expressed through the abrupt transitions in the overall facade treatment.

Left, bottom: An example that well illustrates the eclecticity of this period. The tent-like forms are of a reinforced concrete structure, plastered and painted white. In the plan configuration, each tent structure corresponds to a living space. At the ground level, the spaces are generally open to one another, while at the first level, they are separated to house the bedrooms and bathrooms.

A rather humourous approach to regional architecture is expressed by the overall exterior image. The interior on the other hand is exquisitely and tastefully executed. It utilises the finest workmanship in wood and marble and the very best in furnishings, moulding Eastern and Western decorative motifs to produce spectacular interior spaces. (It is rather unfortunate that I was not permitted to publish any interior photographs, acknowledging the injustice that the exterior does to its interior architecture.)

been initiated to scale down fenestration dimensions.

A more optimistic typology of buildings characterises the Late Post Oil period of the 1980's. On average, the younger generation of today does not have the financial resources available to erect residences that compete in monumentality with those of the earlier period, although one still observes a trend toward eclectic and monumental design. I would like to think of this period as a transitional phase toward more identifiable residential designs. People are becoming more conscious about the functional aspects of traditional dwellings and many young Kuwaitis express concern about the quality of their residential environment. They seem to show more interest in modern designs inspired by tradition. Some are still confused about design aesthetics. Some want "Islamic designs" that they think they can identify with, being disenchanted with the alien international forms but this limited perception only magnifies the problem as the architecture of the Islamic world varies appreciably from one region to another.

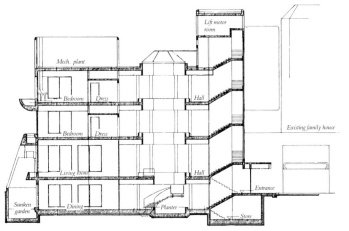

Section AA

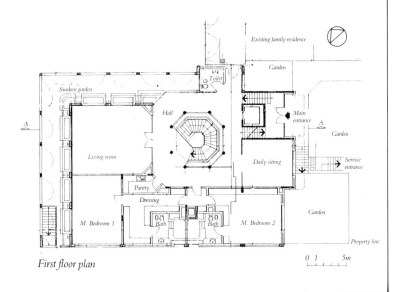

First floor plan

0 1 5m

Al-Marzouk Residence
An example of the Middle Post Oil period. This particular building comprises three independent but connected residences. The image of monumentality is very strongly expressed throughout the structure. Travertine is used as an exterior veneer material. Glass curtain walls, extensive fenestration using double glazed aluminium windows and the arcaded colonnade at the ground level are other characteristic features.

Rather than seek cosmetic architecture, our concern should be to arrive at designs that serve our utilitarian needs in response to our environment in the context of modern living. The fulfillment of our spiritual needs through the embellishment and celebration of building is just as important as utilitarianism. Ornament should be inspired by our culture and should arise from our indigenous vocabulary. The incorporation of architectural genes from alien gene pools is certainly a possibility, but only when it enhances the survival of our architectural organism in the ongoing process of environmental change and evolution.

In attempting to evaluate architectural work which in itself entails artistic or aesthetic expression, one is confronted with the problem of objective versus subjective judgement. As emphasised earlier, utility or the functional aspect of architecture should be the primary objective of design and aesthetic elements are incorporated only to enhance one's architectural identity. Moreover, in the aesthetics of embellishment, objectivity is just an inherent part of architectural evaluation as it is an inherent part of scientific judgement. One has to acknowledge that aesthetic order does exist and it does have underlying principles which have been understood by

many designers throughout history. It is the aesthetic order that has given us the architecture of the past, whether vernacular, monumental or other, that one so much admires and so often wants to replicate or recreate in today's disordered urban environment.

Dr. Roger Scruton, lecturer in philosophy at London University, dismisses the aesthetic idea of "it's all a matter of taste" explaining that people use it to "secure whatever validity they can for their own idiosyncracies". He continues to argue that "In proposing an aesthetics of architecture, the least one must be proposing is an aesthetics of everyday life ...

In one sense it seems aesthetic judgement is subjective — for it consists in the attempt to articulate an individual experience, but in another sense, it is objective for it aims to justify that experience, through presenting reasons that are valid for others besides oneself". And it is this justification that one should be confronted with when evaluating the eclectism of Kuwait's residential forms. One must be responsible to preserve one's architectural identity through uniformly identifiable yet diverse architectural aesthetic concepts and values.

Today it has become extremely difficult to define

an identity for the Kuwaiti house, particularly when one is examining the exterior form of the building. The buildings appear to be designed more as fashionable fads than anything else. Architecture has to be worn and experienced for generations and hence the whimsy can get quite old and aggravating after a while. One simply cannot dispose of buildings every season or every year to allow for designs in vogue! Some people might have a more relaxed attitude toward the residential architecture carnival in Kuwait. Charles Jencks, in his "Dream houses of Los Angeles" describes the eclectic houses as having "an immediate sensual quality, an ability to make you turn your head away from the traffic, look and however reluctantly smile ... even if it isn't the High Game of serious architecture, it is nonetheless a form of enjoyment, erotic in its self-obsession". Although not said in the Kuwaiti context, this attitude should not be adopted to encourage architecture toward that objective. The architectural joke gets stale after

a while and eventually will become a source of discomfort and annoyance for the user, his neighbours and anyone who has to experience it on a continuous basis.

Although the environment is constantly changing, the societies and cultures are forever evolving, civilisations nevertheless are always built on the foundations of the past. One

learns from history and the past offers a reservoir of solutions and approaches that one can still adapt. The design intention however, is not to replicate the architecture of the past but to respect its concepts and to perpetuate a relation between the past, the present and the future in an attempt to further develop and preserve a national architectural identity

"A good place is one which, in some way
appropriate to the person and her
culture, makes her aware of her
community, her past, the web of life,
and the universe of time and space
in which those are contained."
Bachelard

144

Late Post Oil period
1980's

Left: An architectural experiment in the use of pseudo-classical design vocabulary. It portrays yet another palatial image that strives for monumentality, a design trend that continues to prevail into this period.

Left, below: A modern architectural statement of the Late Post Oil period. The facade rejects use of historic cliches. The articulation of volumes, masses and elevation elements are pure responses to functional requirements. Concrete is used as a facade material, its mass broken by the volumetric elevations and the recessed fenestration.

Right: The overall relative simplicity of the elevations and the uncomplicated articulation of facade elements are characteristic of the changes that have taken place over the years, although an image of monumentality is still expressed. Other noticeable features include the absence of balconies, the use of concrete, a more durable material than plaster, as a veneer for the facade and the extensive use of arched fenestration utilising aluminium frames.

Right: The trend towards eclectic and monumental design is still observed in this Late Post Oil period example. The exterior has been inspired by Muslim Spain and North African palatial architecture.

Below: An architect's free style interpretation of modern classicism is illustrated here. The absence of balconies, the overall reduction in fenestration and the use of limestone as a more durable facade material are other characteristic features.

Below, right: A "free style" pseudo-Islamic revival of the Late Post Oil period. Disenchanted with alien international forms, another cosmetic approach to architecture is chosen within an interpretation of traditional design. The wind towers which were rare in Kuwait's traditional dwellings are in this example made of concrete and used for purely visual purposes.

Abdul-Latif Al-Hamad's Residence

An unusual example of the late 1960's that utilises the traditional courtyard concept. The social aspect of the courtyard can still be provided for in today's residential designs through the incorporation of the enclosed courtyard, exemplified by this residence. Here, the overall design motifs exhibit North African influences, particularly Moroccan, portrayed by the screened doors and windows, the arcades and the lanterns in the loggia. The colourful cushions used for the floor seating are handwoven and embroidered of Northern Iraqi origin. The loggia, surrounding the courtyard and leading into the other living spaces is used to display some very fine works of art. The overall interior space composition is dynamic and exciting.

The first time visitor is always intrigued and happily surprised upon entering this space as the calm and modest exterior, well hidden in vegetation, reveals little of the interior. The main living room houses the finest Damascene antique furniture. The intricate geometric and floral designs in wood are ornately inlaid with mother-of-pearl, each piece, being a work of art in itself.

Abdulla Al-Dakhil's Residence

One of the few examples featured here that discards historic cliches and cosmetic architecture. It presents an optimistic and an unpretentious typology of residential design. The exterior utilises brick, a locally manufactured material, as a veneer element. The windows are set into arcaded concrete canopies and employ wood shutters. The overall facade treatment is well proportioned and displays an appealing and a soothing image amidst the existing hodge-podge of architectural manifestations.

The daily living room facing the swimming pool and garden. Modular floor cushions are used to create a comfortable interior space that reflects a harmonious blend of modern and traditional elements. Brass trays are used as tables for the floor seating and the Afghani carpet adds colour and coherence to the overall composition.

Al-Mas'oud Residence

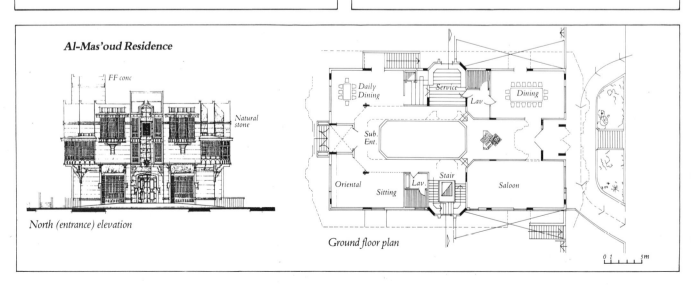

North (entrance) elevation

Ground floor plan

0 1   5m

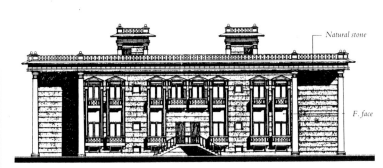

West elevation

Natural stone
F. face

Natural stone
F. face

South elevation (Entrance facade)

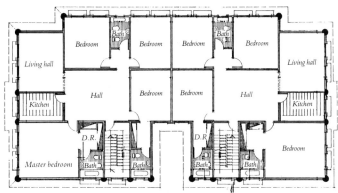

First floor plan

Ground floor plan

Al-Adwani Residence

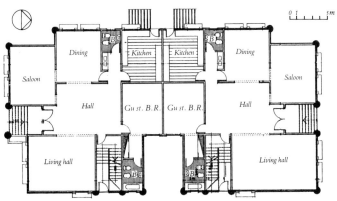

0 1   5m

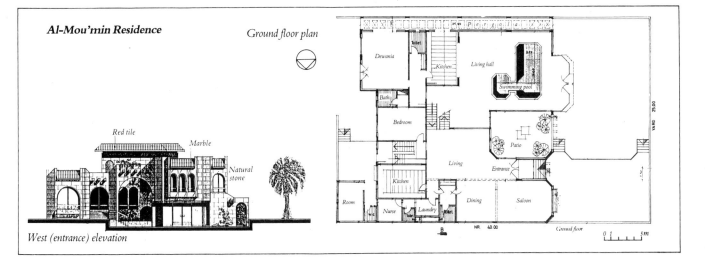

Al-Mou'min Residence

Ground floor plan

Red tile

Marble

Natural stone

West (entrance) elevation

Ground floor

0 1   5m

Hamad Al-Bahar's Residence

The Oriental room, a typical interior space seen in many of Kuwait's modern residences. This particular room opens into a reception hall that has been furnished in a European, (mostly French) style.

The wall panelling in wood, the seating and the upholstery are all locally made. The large brass trays used as tables are of Pakistani origin. Antique Persian rugs are used both on the floor, over the fitted carpet, and on the wall, over the wood panelling to accentuate the Oriental composition.

Huda H. Al-Bahar is a Kuwaiti architect who has been educated in the U.S. She works at the Kuwait Institute for Scientific Research and is presently involved in doctoral research at the Bartlett School of Architecture, London University.

A Note on the General Organisation of Space

The traditional courtyard house has been discarded as a design alternative in most of Kuwait's modern villas. Today, the private villa is sited on a lot that varies in size between 500 square metres to 1000 square metres. It is detached structure having no party walls except perhaps for the fence which always surrounds the garden around the house. Space can generally be divided into two broad categories: private and public. The private space comprises the bedrooms and bathrooms, a daily living room, a small kitchen and perhaps a small dining room and it is normally situated on the upper storey of the building. The lower storey public space consists of one or more guest living rooms, and an "Arabic" room is occasionally included, a guest dining room, a guest washroom and sometimes a guest bedroom and bath. The main kitchen is rarely used by the housewife, as most households rely on cooks for meal preparation. Quite often the main kitchen is located close to the guest dining room area on the lower level, although at times, the kitchen is built as a detached structure outside the main residential building. Unlike the popular use of roofs for various social functions in the traditional buildings of Kuwait, the modern roofs no longer have a social function; they are merely used to house air-conditioning equipment, water storage tanks and often a laundry room.

The *diwan*, or social gathering place for men, is still a desired space, although it is incorporated in only a few of today's residential designs. Quite often, the *diwan* is built as an independent structure in the garden of the residence and more popular in use are those which exist independently on a separate land lot, detached and often not related in design to the dwelling. In such cases, each extended family would have its own *diwan* named after it. The *diwans* vary in size and spatial configuration although they are almost always on one level. The larger ones have several living rooms, a dining area, a kitchen and guest accommodations. Moreover, as most families rely on servants for various household services, servants quarters are always incorporated in the design. They are usually built as independent units in one corner of the garden.

Unlike the plethora of exterior architectural styles and motifs, domestic space organisation does not vary significantly from one house to another. The basic space functions and their relation to one another (already discussed), are usually present in similar forms. Some of the recent plans, however, incorporate a courtyard design and a few of the residences are designed as one storey buildings. Finally, it is significant to note that interior eclectism is more apparent in the furniture and furnishings rather than in the spaces themselves.

Modern, ultra modern, high tech, French of various periods, other European, Far Eastern, Arabic, Bedouin and other styles can all be seen, and a variety is often present in a single residence where each living space is of a different style.

A Note on Structure and Materials

Most of Kuwait's modern residential architecture is constructed primarily of a reinforced concrete structure, utilising flab slabs for floors and roofs and concrete blocks for walls and partitions. The exterior is either plastered or often veneered with brick or stone (be it marble, travertine, sandstone or limestone) or various configurations and textures of precast or cast in place concrete veneer elements.

The brick commonly used is produced in Kuwait whereas stone is always imported commonly from Jordan, Lebanon, Saudi Arabia, Greece and Italy. Wood is scarcely used except for some interior spaces, doors, window shutters and quite infrequently window frames. This has been due to its expense and the severe warping that it undergoes in the harsh Kuwaiti climate.

Roofs are frequently flat although different forms of pitched and tiled roofs are becoming increasingly popular. Windows are almost always of aluminium frame, whether rectangular, arched or circular in nature, and most are manufactured locally.

Bohra Houses OF Gujarat

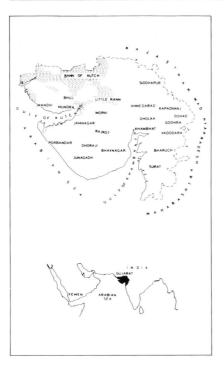

Article by Balkrishna Doshi based on research by the Vastu-Silpa Foundation. Photographs and drawings courtesy of the author.

Above, left: Map of Gujarat locating Bohra settlements.
Above: Entrance gateway to one of the Bohravads.

The Bohra settlements and houses of Gujarat, in western India, present an architectural response of an exposure to another culture and a desire to maintain one's own identity. Traditionally, the Bohras are primarily engaged in trade, conducting business with Burma, the Zanzibar Islands and the Arab world. They first settled in the port town of Khambat in Gujarat and spread to other towns in Gujarat such as Surat, Kapadvanj, Dohad, Godhra, Vadodra, Siddhpur, Dholka, Patan, etc. As the Bohras grew in number, they began to form in each settlement their own distinct neighbourhood called a *Bohravad*. Today Bohràs number more than a million and have settled both in India and abroad.

Essentially, Bohravads fall into two different categories based on their physical layout: One, an organic development characteristic of the traditional city pattern of this region and two, a gridiron layout. However, both these developments still maintain a closed-system of streets, sub-streets and small open spaces accessible only through a gate linking to the city streets and the overall urban fabric.

Almost all the Bohravads which are more than 100 years old, have evolved organically within the confines of the available land in the fortified city. The newer Bohravads which generally occur adjacent to an old one or on the fringe of the settlements have evolved due to the Bhoras' contacts with the Europeans and travel abroad. These are laid out in gridiron pattern and are not constrained by the shape and size of the land.

Like the neighbourhoods of other communities, buildings for the various religious and cultural activities of the Bohra community also occur within the domain of the Bohravad. These buildings include a mosque, the assembly hall for religious discourse, the local priest's house, a travellers' lodge and a community hall for ceremonial occasions, especially the commensal dinners.

In order to understand the architectural forms of the Bohravad and its houses, it is essential to understand the contextual frame and religious plurality in which they live in Gujarat. In practice, the Bohras refer to themselves as "Bohras". This characteristic reflects the way they maintain a separate identity.

The house of a Bohra is a shelter for security, collective living and human hierarchy. There are three kinds of architectural forms in which the identity of the Bohras is manifested: commercial buildings, religious buildings, and residential buildings. In commercial areas, the architectural forms more or less symbolise the common regional characteristics of the trading communities of Gujarat with rows of shops on the ground floor on either side of the street.

Neighbourhood plan and a typical street facade, Ahmedabad.

In the bazaar, it would be difficult to identify a Bohra shop from any other shop except for the physical appearance of a Bohra, who stands out because of his dress, or the signboard.

The religious places include a mosque, a hall, a priest's house, a tomb and a cemetery. These distinctly reflect the Bohra identity by the way of strong geometrical forms are woven with the local designs making the whole facade very ornamental and decorative. It is strongly reflected in their mosque and tomb. The use of a community hall for collective fasting, feasting, marriage and meetings makes it an active place for continuous collective interaction.

The Bohra houses reflect three interesting features.

• The hierarchy maintained in the Bohra's life is found in their houses by way of vertical and horizontal hierarchy of its spaces, going from the most public to the most private enclosures.

• The enclosed spaces within the house also reflect their efforts to maintain a distinct identity from other religious groups and a sense of seclusion and privacy from outsiders.

• As many of their houses are built above their shops or in separate Bohravads, this provides a degree of security against outsiders. At the same time, these houses do not open directly on the front street, and thereby preclude the possibility of quick access into the houses. Even after the entry, the principle of hierarchy is maintained by way of a vertical hierarchy in the house. It is for this reason that the close relatives are entertained in the first floor *ordo* (family room).

House

A typical Bohra house is distinguished by its facade decor, the treatment of the openings and rich materials of construction. Apart from a typical space use pattern identifying the private and semi-public domain, the basic plan of a Bohra house is found to be very similar to that of a Hindu house which conforms to the general pattern of a medieval row house. In a Bohra dwelling the typical space organisation is as described below.

At the ground level one enters the house through a portico raised about 75 centimetres above the street level. Through the main door, one steps into an anteroom, known as *dehli* separated by a light screen from the inner court to ensure privacy inside the house. This space usually houses a stair which directly leads to the upper floors. From here visitors are directly led up to the formal sitting room on the first floor. Next the court, open to the sky, houses all the services on its side walls.

The space immediately after the court is fully open on the courtside and referred to as *baharni parsal* (external portico). This is followed by a room known as *andarni parsal* (internal portico). Such seemingly incongruous designation of these spaces is with reference to the last room of the house, the *ordo* (family room), which is the sanctum of a Bohra family's life. For all practical purposes, on the ground floor, the Bohra family uses the spaces beyond the inner court and the space immediately following the court becomes an external portico, followed by an inner portico and then the family room.

The upper floors are normally organised as independent rooms on either sides of the court around which the services are located. In the case of a house with more than one upper floor, the stair is also located in the area around the court. This space is known as *ravas*. On the top floor, the *ravas* becomes a terrace separating the rooms in the front and at the back. A double lean-to roof over both these rooms allows an attic space underneath known as *daglo*.

Use of spaces

Contrary to the other communities, the Bohras rarely use the raised, street side portico, which is used extensively by other communities for various activities such as sitting space for elders and play area for children. This could be attributed to the greater confinement of women in the social set up of the Bohras.

Once inside, the anteroom serves as the second buffer between the inner and external domain. Generally, light wooden screens are placed to avoid a clear view into the house from the street. This also serves as a brief meeting point between the menfolk and casual visitors. The staircase to the first floor is located here and directly leads the guests to the first floor sitting room. On the ground floor, beyond the anteroom, is the family domain into which only the close relatives and family friends are invited.

The open to sky court helps ventilate the whole house besides letting in light on all floors. The kitchen and other services are located around the court. The court as well as the *baharni parsal* are used for dining and lounging and all domestic activities are also carried out here. *Bethak* — a large wooden platform with storage underneath and a soft cushion on the top — is the dominant piece of furniture in this space. These spaces actually are the hub of the family world and used throughout the day. Next, the *andarni parsal,* being covered, extends the use in monsoon when the court is unusable.

Andarni parsal often has a swing which is popular in hot climates to keep cool. This space is used predominantly as a family lounging space during the hot afternoons. Beyond it the house ends in the family's living room *ordo,* which is richly decorated with seating in traditional style placed on the floor. The cupboard on the extreme rear wall of this room is always designed in Islamic traditions representing the concept of nine squares known as *navkhand*. Such a cupboard with intricate carvings is an inseparable component of a Dawoodi's house. This space is used to entertain relatives, and family friends and for sleeping.

Generally a service lane separates the next parallel row houses. This barely ensures ventilation and natural illumination is extremely low in this room on the ground floor.

The first floor is reached by a stair from the anteroom at the ground floor. From the first floor upwards, the stair is often provided near the court, allowing for an independent use of the rooms on either side. A large room at the back on this level is generally used as a formal living area and guests are entertained here. The windows mostly have double shutters, one of wood and the other of stained glass. The room in the front is used as a multi-purpose space and sometimes has a covered balcony.

Construction and building materials

Comprised of bays in a row house system, the structure of a typical Bohra house is simple. Each bay is about 5 metres wide bordered on the longer sides by walls shared by the adjoining units.

The construction up to plinth is in stone which protects the house from the damp rising from the ground and also provides a base for the facade. The superstructure in most cases is executed as a system of frame structures in wood with brick masonry infill walls. The floors are supported on wooden beams spanning across the bay and, where the load is heavier, supported by additional wooden posts. All the wooden posts sit on stone bases to avoid decay from dampness. Wooden posts in the line of the bay walls are encased in the brick masonry infill wall.

Upper floors are constructed by resting closely, smaller sections of wooden members on the beams spanning the bay walls, which support either a stone or bamboo mat surface on which the bed mortar is laid. This is finished with the desired flooring material. The roofing is of galvanized iron sheets

View of a mosque in Siddhpur, revealing a decorative facade influenced by the British.

resting on beams directly spanning the width of the bay.

Decor

As noted earlier, the basic space structure of a Bohra house is quite similar to that of the other communities in the region. It is to a large extent the decor that sets them apart from these other houses.

The Hindu houses are by and large found to be quite plain in their treatment of facades as well as elements like columns, elaborately patterned false ceilings, wooden furniture with floral scrolls, painted and etched window glasses, etc. Elaborate carpets and rugs are a common feature of Bohra houses and occur rarely in a Hindu house. Bohras being a quite successful trading community, could afford such elaborate decor and, it was natural for the houses to reflect it. It is also no surprise that the Bohras should adopt a style and the elements of decor which were used by the British in the design of their buildings. The Bohras did business with them and must have looked upon the British decor as the thing to identify with and aspire to.

A study of the decorative motifs, especially in false ceilings and window panes, reveals that these are not strictly geometric patterns but also contain representational motifs such as the floral patterns. In the facades, a great variety was observed from among the various European styles in the treatment of components such as doors, windows, columns, and balustrades. Arched openings such as the flat, the semicircular, the segmental, and the pointed are

observed. Columns are found to vary from simple regional designs to variations of the Greek classical order.

Even when executed in a more regional style, the façades are generally picturesque and show an approach to total design which is not found in other houses of the same period.

Some preliminary observations

Bohra houses have naturally evolved in the context of the region and its traditional habitat pattern. Being Hindu converts, this evolution appears to have been a slow process of modifying organisation of space and objects, and elements of daily use, within the social values and beliefs of their new religion.

This process of evolution has been more additive in nature, particularly in the basic plan of the house and the arrangement of the groups. The changes occurred in the decor and elements of interior spaces and furniture which acquired sophistication in design and detailing. This is easily noticeable in the latter-day house facades, furniture and fixtures, treatment of openings, internal partitions and false ceilings. This superimposition of external and internal changes on the basic plan can be attributed to the British influence on the Bohra community due to their trade relationships and an exposure to the British lifestyle in Europe.

The form and structure of a Bohra house is similar to the Hindu house, all rooms occur along a single axis of movement, leaving only the last room free of the general movement which can

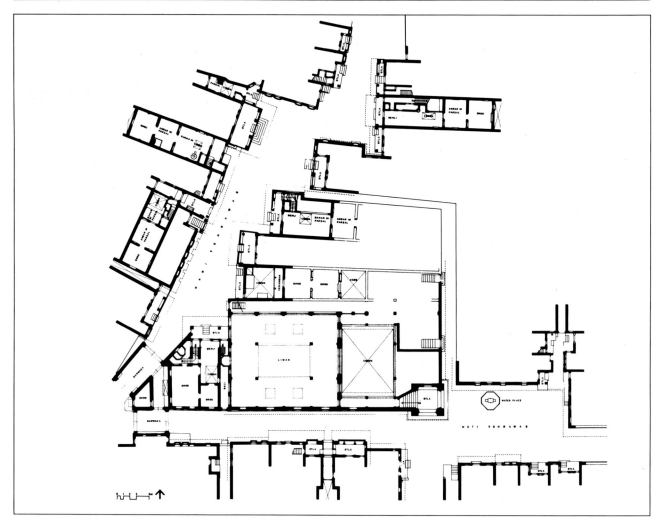

Above: Plan, Vohrawads, Kapadvang.
Right: Plan, Religious Complex, Siddhpur.

be used without disturbance. This indicates the low priority given to degree of privacy within the family unlike the colonial house. Privacy vis-a-vis outsiders is of greater concern to Bohras than Hindus. And this is indicated by a screen between the internal court and anteroom, from where the visitors are directly led upstairs to the formal sitting room. Apart from these minor, localised additions, the basic plan organisation remains the same as its Hindu origin.

Even when opportunities were available, as in the case of the house of Taherbhai Madraswala at Siddhpur (see drawing), there is no effort at evolving a more sophisticated plan in spite of its larger width and location facilitating three open sides. As a result even such a large house becomes 'twice' the traditional house. It appears that the strong colonial influence is only manifested in the decor of the interiors and the furniture for identity purpose

152

Above: Street facade.
Above, right: Richly decorated entrance to a house.

only to express their contact with the external world which dealt in business and economic status. Yet, basically the inner requirements of the Bohras remained the same.

Facades

It is in facades that the Bohra houses, built early this century, differ from the Hindu houses as well as that of the initial converts. It is in these facades that the variations of European styles become dominant. In Siddhpur, the most interesting and conspicuously significant features are the houses with their eclectic façades. Though derived from simple modules and bays of a plan, the houses present a complex exterior. European in appearance, they far from reflect the lifestyles of those who live within. These facades are a mixture of many styles, from many places and periods. Fanciful forms of Renaissance and Baroque styles are freely used to decorate the sculpturesque elements, particularly columns, pilasters and entablatures. An effect of great richness is produced by integrating the mouldings with the capitals, decorated panels, deep cornices, iron grills, and wooden doorworks. The combining of many styles reveals the eclectic effect more as rhetoric than as a genuine concern for giving expression to a style of architecture. Surprisingly, the facades do not display any Islamic characteristics except for a sense of privacy that pervades

the interior and the lack of figurative use of any living beings — man or animal — as part of the decorations.

The houses stand out for their style of grafting all sorts of details on a rather functional and simple plan. There is a total disregard for regional, local or traditional forms as far as appearance is concerned. However, there is an inexplicable Indian-ness about the pseudo-European Renaissance and Baroque facades due to the environment and the builders. The house fronts are profusely ornamented and even when relatively plain, they have a sculpturesque quality and exhibit, to a greater or lesser degree, an irrational and unsanctified use of the classical elements. The style leans towards being 'manneristic' which at times is disturbing, restless and confused. The force behind the facade decoration seems to be of contrived effects, which are at once dramatic and rich. Expressions which are often associated with ecclesiastical buildings are used on secular buildings.

The decorations extend over the entire facade, differing from house to house in form as well as colour. However, a very definite control is achieved by the interrelation of key elements such as floor heights, plinths, and the roof line; other smaller elements are used to harmonise and bind the entire facade. The colour renderings are in pastel shades with light green, light yellow and pink as favourites. The materials used are a combination of stone, wood and plaster. The entire facade is

busy. Between the pilasters are placed the doorway, the windows and the decorated panels. The wood and iron grillwork is used for the door and windows, their shutters consisting of smaller parts and operating separately and helping to retain privacy. On areas such as the wall below the sill of a window — there are no openings — plastered decorative panels are placed. The decorations are in the nature of European shields or plaques with flowers and ribbons and the names of the owners; the date of construction is written in darker shades below.

In conclusion, it can be said that over the centuries, Bohras have definitely evolved a house characteristic which is largely distinct from that of other houses in the region. The space use pattern, the treatment of the façades and the decor are characteristically different from Hindu houses. The Bohras, in their search for a separate identity, judiciously utilised elements of European architecture via the British influence. However, the influences have only been skin deep. No radical changes took place in the Bohra's social values and religious beliefs. This being reflected in their habitat, which basically remains the same as the Hindu one of their origin, illustrates the strong adherence to their traditional way of life and thought. Bohra settlements and houses are a unique phenomenon and demonstrate a balance between harmony and variety, and between something private and public. It provides us with an instructive lesson in urban design.

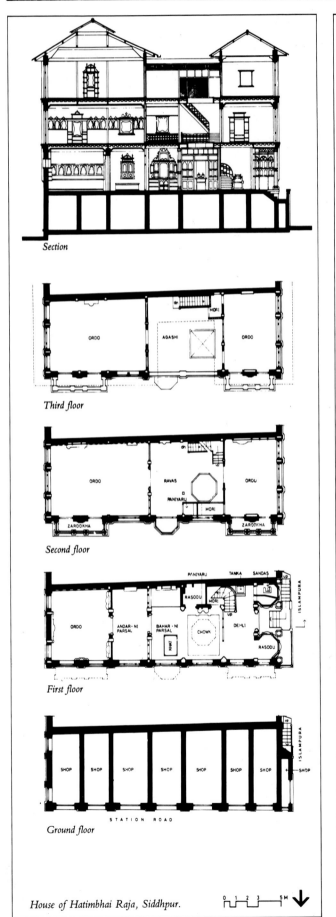

Section

Third floor

Second floor

First floor

Ground floor

House of Hatimbhai Raja, Siddhpur.

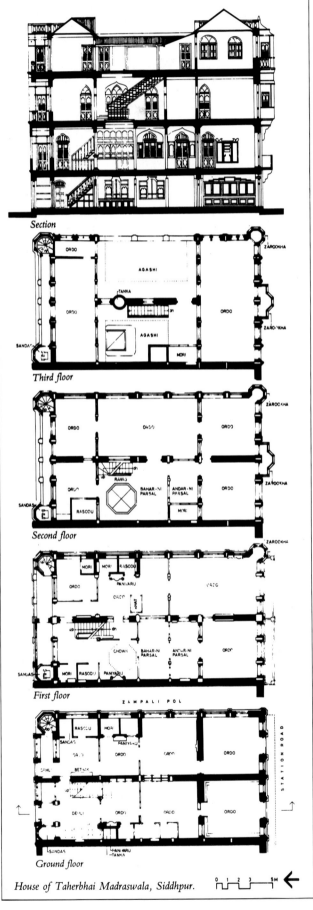

Section

Third floor

Second floor

First floor

Ground floor

House of Taherbhai Madraswala, Siddhpur.

Far left: Andarni Parsal, with a swing in the foreground.
Left: An elaborate drinking-water storage area.
Far left, below: Detail of a wooden column with its richly carved decoration.
Left, below: View of an internal court and staircase.
Left, bottom: The family room, ordo, of an affluent Bohra.

Balkrishna Doshi, one of India's foremost architects, wrote this article based on research carried out by the Vastu-Silpa Foundation in Ahmedabad, under a grant from the Aga Khan Program at Harvard and MIT. The article has been edited for publication by Akhtar Badshah.

THE KAZAK YURT

The yurt[1] is a tent that is almost a house; though it is as portable as any tent. The shape of the yurt is close to that of the dome, the dwelling form that encloses the maximum volume with a minimum of surface area. Outside, the winds slip easily around and over this aerodynamic shape. Inside, the circular walls and upward sloping roof give to the interior a feeling of great space. The framework supports itself, no poles stand inside, and no stakes are needed outside (an advantage when pitching the yurt on frozen ground). The interior is kept warm in the coldest weather by adding layers of thick wool felt to the walls; in the summer, the sides can be rolled up to admit cooling breezes.

A yurt can be put up or taken down in less than an hour. Loaded on the backs of two camels, bullocks, or yaks, it travels anywhere in steppe, desert, or mountain country. Because the yurt frame is self-supporting, it can be moved without taking it down: to clean house, the yurt is picked up and moved to a new spot.

Unlike so many tents that have all but disappeared in the face of industrialisation and westernisation, the yurt is still in use. (In the yurt's Mongolian homeland, three quarters of the population still live in yurts, many of them factory produced.) A good yurt costs the average worker only two to three months' wages, and many yurts now have stoves, electricity, and wooden floors. The yurt adapted easily to these conveni-

[1] The word "yurt" is Turkic for "dwelling".

ences: the stove sits in the centre, the traditional hearth place; a stovepipe carries the smoke to the smoke hole which is covered with clear plastic to let in light and keep out the cold.

The yurt is found over an area that stretches from the Caspian Sea, along southern Russia, through Mongolia, and up into Siberia. This is the land of the great Central Asian Steppe, an area of little rainfall, fierce winds, and cold winters. Across this territory are spread Mongol- and Turkish-speaking nomads, descendants of the great Mongol Hordes who built an empire that stretched from China to Europe.

The steppe tribes that dwell in yurts may be divided into two groups according to the type of yurt they use (this division was first proposed in 1896 by the Russian ethnographer Charusin). The Mongol or Kalmuck yurt is used by the Mongol, Altian, Buriat, and Tatar tribes of the east and the Kalmuck tribes of the west, most of which speak a Mongol-derived language. The yurt used by these people has straight roof poles making the roof a cone. The Kirgiz or Turkic yurt has a curve in the roof poles which makes the roof into a dome. It is used by the Turkic-speaking people to the west, the Kirgiz, Kazaks, Uzbeks, and Turkmen. In addition to the roof shape there are other characteristics that tend to go with each style.

Yurt Construction

The yurt and felt are both inventions of Central Asia. Feltmaking is an ancient craft (historically preceding spinning and weaving) and a simple process: wool is fluffed, spread out on a reed mat, moistened, and

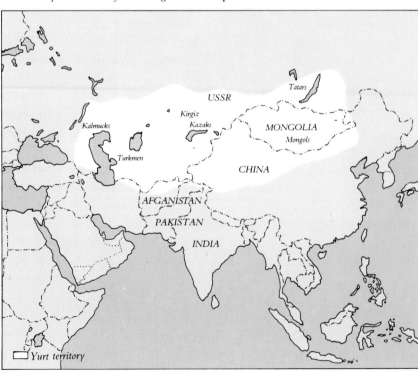

Yurt territory

Text and drawings by Torvald Faegre are taken from his book "Tents, Architecture of the Nomads".

The yurt is unquestionably one of the greatest inventions Asia has brought forth. Its circular structure and dome-like roof combine the maximum structure with extraordinary stability. During my stay in the Pamirs the heaviest storms raged over the aul[1] without a moments cessation all through January, yet never once was one yurt blown down.

Gustav Krist, *Alone Through the Forbidden Land.*

[1]*Yurt camp.*

Interior decoration of a yurt.

rolled and beaten again and again until the fibres mat together. In Asia, felt is used for hats, outer garments, boots, and rugs, as well as a cover for dwellings. This material is unsurpassed as protection against cold, wind, and rain. As many as eight layers of felt may cover a yurt in the winter, and sometimes the top layer is oiled to help water run off. But felt has one deficiency — it has little tensile strength and can be easily pulled apart. Therefore, a felt-covered structure must be self-supporting; it cannot rely on the felt to hold up the poles as with the black tents of Arabia.

The Frame

The yurt was created to provide a portable framework to support a felt-tent cover. In addition, the frame had to be made of materials found in wood-scarce regions where the poles are not large. One advantage of the yurt is that the frame does not use poles of any great diameter. Willow suits these requirements perfectly; it is tough and grows plentifully in the steppe areas. The wall sections of the yurt are made of willow rods an inch or less in diameter, split in half, and criss-crossed over one another with hinged joints of knotted rawhide. Not only does this make walls portable, but the diagonal direction of the slats increase the strength and stability of the walls. A roof pole is tied at each criss-cross at the top of the walls. At their top ends the roof poles socket into a bent circle of wood, the crown. A simple conical roof can be constructed of roof poles joined at the top, tipi style, but the crown allows for shorter roof poles and creates an unencumbered hole for smoke and light.

The roof and walls are now tied together but will not stand permanently. Left alone, the roof poles will push the wall sections back, unfolding them to the ground. For this reason, a woven band is tied around the top of the wall. This "tension band" is the keystone of the yurt; all the compressive forces that push outward are held inward by this band. Some yurt dwellers honour the function of this band by weaving it with intricate patterns that denote a particular

family, clan or tribe just as their rugs do.

In size the Kazak yurts vary widely depending on the tribe and wealth of the family. The small yurts of the poor may only be ten feet in diameter while those of the wealthy can be twenty feet or more. All of the wooden parts of these yurts use naturally shaped willow rods and saplings with a minimum of cutting and joinery. This gives these components superior strength because they are used whole or are split and not sawed (the saw always cuts across some grain weakening the wood).

The roof poles are cut green, soaked,

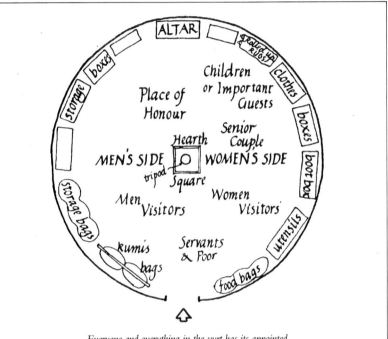

Everyone and everything in the yurt has its appointed place. There is a women's side and a men's side. There is a "place of honour," a spot on the men's side in back of the hearth — away from the cold. The young and sometimes animal newborn sit close to the door. Saddles, guns, and ropes are placed on the men's side, while the churn, kitchen tools and the cradle sit on the women's side. The yurt is traditionally set up by women, although men may assist. A bride's dowry usually included a yurt. Traditional nomad hospitality required that anyone stopping outside a yurt would be welcomed in for a meal. A lamb or sheep would be killed and there would be a feast.

debarked, and then heated at one end and bent to shape. The natural taper of the sapling makes a perfect roof pole, since the poles should be thinner toward the top for maximum strength and minimum weight. In some areas the poles are charred slightly to make them impervious to insects. In Afghanistan a yurt frame treated in this manner will last forty to fifty years. The crown is manufactured by bending two split saplings in a semicircle and fastening them together with rawhide or metal hoops. Across the crown are fastened wood rods bent in a concave curve to hold the smoke flap up. Each tribe has its own par-

ticular configuration of these rods; from inside the yurt they make a striking pattern against the sky.

The door frame is commonly made from juniper wood — light but tough and weather resistant. Many Kirgiz-style yurts have carved wooden doors (attached with rope hinges), but felt doors, which can be rolled up when not in use, are more common. Many yurts in the southern areas use reed mats for wall coverings — these afford privacy, keep out animals, and let air circulate in the summertime. In the wintertime felt is added under the mats and the wall mats may be plastered to make them windproof. The felt covering on these yurts often have felt applique designs sewn on the borders. The felt is bound to the tent with ropes and cords that cross the roof and walls in symmetrical patterns.

Inside the yurt

As one enters a yurt it is considered impolite to step on the threshold or touch the tent ropes. The floor is covered with a thin felt rug in the summer. In the winter, a layer of felt is put down, then covered with four inches of dried grass, and topped with felt rugs. In the centre a space is left for the hearth. Four boards form the hearth square and an iron tripod holds the cooking pots. Charcoal is burned where available, but more often there is only dried dung for fuel — the roof becomes blackened with its acrid smoke. Sometimes a stove was built of adobe with an iron plate top, but today sheet iron stoves are preferred. These have a stovepipe so that the smoke hole can be closed with a plastic sheet to keep the heat in.

The door always faces south or southeast, away from the prevailing winds. Opposite the doorway sits a chest that in pre-revolutionary times was the family shrine where Buddhist images sat with brass butter lamps and offering bowls. Nowadays, family photos and transistor radios have taken over this spot. Around the walls are placed chests, bags, and rolled up carpets. Decorative cloths hang from the walls and may be suspended as curtains to divide the yurt.

The tent is regarded as a sanctified shelter under the protection of which life proceeds. All clan deliberations and gatherings take place in the tent by which the Kirgiz swear: "I swear upon my tent".

Waldemar Jochelson, *Peoples of Asiatic Russia.*

Decorative bands inside the yurt (applique and embroidery).

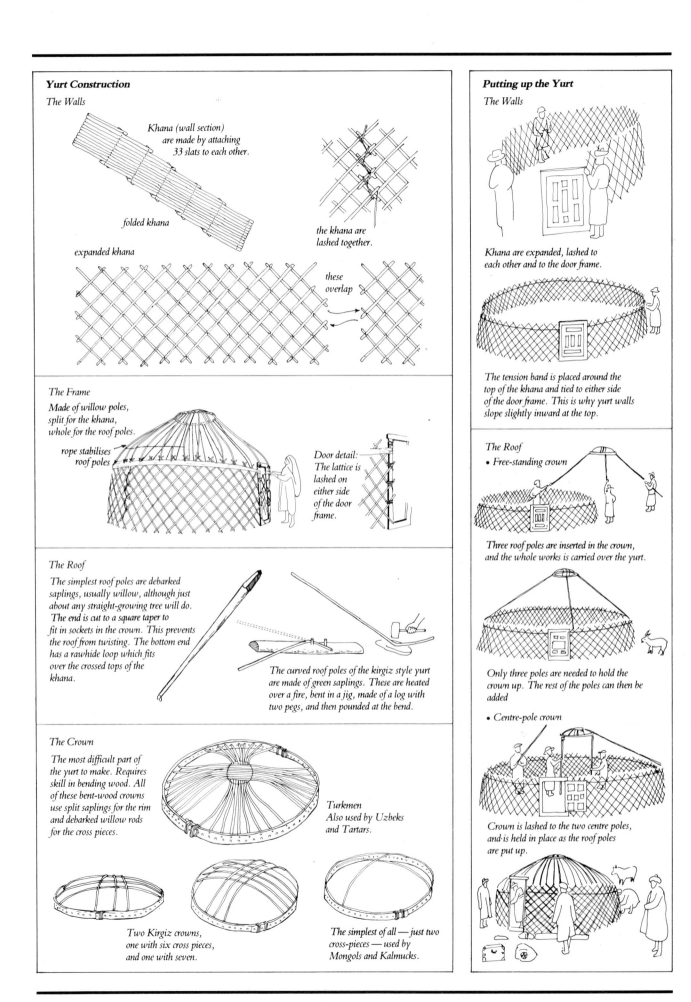

Yurt Construction

The Walls

Khana (wall section) are made by attaching 33 slats to each other.

folded khana

expanded khana

the khana are lashed together.

these overlap

The Frame

Made of willow poles, split for the khana, whole for the roof poles.

rope stabilises roof poles

Door detail: The lattice is lashed on either side of the door frame.

The Roof

The simplest roof poles are debarked saplings, usually willow, although just about any straight-growing tree will do. The end is cut to a square taper to fit in sockets in the crown. This prevents the roof from twisting. The bottom end has a rawhide loop which fits over the crossed tops of the khana.

The curved roof poles of the kirgiz style yurt are made of green saplings. These are heated over a fire, bent in a jig, made of a log with two pegs, and then pounded at the bend.

The Crown

The most difficult part of the yurt to make. Requires skill in bending wood. All of these bent-wood crowns use split saplings for the rim and debarked willow rods for the cross pieces.

Turkmen
Also used by Uzbeks and Tartars.

Two Kirgiz crowns, one with six cross pieces, and one with seven.

The simplest of all — just two cross-pieces — used by Mongols and Kalmucks.

Putting up the Yurt

The Walls

Khana are expanded, lashed to each other and to the door frame.

The tension band is placed around the top of the khana and tied to either side of the door frame. This is why yurt walls slope slightly inward at the top.

The Roof

• Free-standing crown

Three roof poles are inserted in the crown, and the whole works is carried over the yurt.

Only three poles are needed to hold the crown up. The rest of the poles can then be added

• Centre-pole crown

Crown is lashed to the two centre poles, and·is held in place as the roof poles are put up.

Left: Designs on straw curtain (plaited).
Left, below: Hearth felt (applique).

Mr. Faegre is a carpenter, currently rehabilitating old buildings in Chicago. The colour reproductions are taken from "A Collection of the Kazak Folk Arrt Designs", courtesy of the Xinjiang People's Publishing House.

Courtyard Houses

C H I N A

There was a double motivation which led us across China from East to West: from Beijing to Kashi; we were in search of the rural habitat on one hand, and of the traces of Islam on the other. It was fascinating to visit the urban communes in Beijing, then to observe the size and the life of the neighbourhood around the Great Mosque in Xi'an, and ultimately to plunge into Central Asia along the Silk Route to the towns of Urümqi, Turfan, and Kashi where the Uygur populations of Xinjiang reside, more than three and a half thousand kilometres from Beijing, among very different ethnic groups who spoke a form of Turkish, in a landscape of desert steppes. We could have easily forgotten that we were still in China. From Beijing to Turfan, from temperate areas across the loess plateaux to arid deserts, northern China shares a number of similarities: hot summers, harsh winters, minimal precipitation and violent winds. The average temperatures in Beijing range from 4°C in January to 26°C in July, and in Turfan, from 10°C to 32°C; as for rainfall, it amounts to 630 mm a year in Beijing, and drops to less than 250 mm in Xinjiang.

At the risk of generalising, one can nonetheless venture to state several characteristic traits of dwelling architecture: the enclosure of spaces behind imposing protective walls; the presence of spaces for outdoor activities inseparable from the dwelling itself; finally, the nearly constant use of earth as a material for construction. This latter point is not at all surprising, since the word *jianzhu* (architecture) incorporates the word *zhu* which is also employed for pisé (or rammed earth). Another observation which applies to all of the regions visited is that rural construction in general is of the highest quality, be it in the organisation of

Above: The detailing is elegant. The decorative opening at the top allows hot air to escape and the two rows of tiles prevent the rain from eroding the wall. Photograph: H.U. Khan.

Top: In a typical village (the one shown here is some forty kilometres from Xi'an), the houses are grouped in rows, creating pleasing rhythms of easily identifiable entrances. Photograph: P. Clément.

Left: The entrance to the house at the boundary wall still retains its traditional character — with "curled-up" edges which now have dragon symbols instead of representational sculptures. Photograph: H.U. Khan.

Text by Pierre Clément.

Commune House near Xi'an

This commune on the outskirt of the city is quite rich as evidenced by the house of a communist party factory worker and his extended family.

Right: The house viewed from the entrance — the main living area is to the rear (painted blue), to the right are two bedrooms for the extended family. The structure under construction, on the left, is for additional bedrooms. Photograph: H.U. Khan.

Below, right: View of the courtyard looking towards the entrance. The bedrooms are to the left. The structure to the right of the entrance is an animal pen. Photograph: H.U. Khan.

Below: The entrance to the house is whitewashed while the walls remain untreated. Photograph: H.U. Khan.

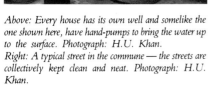

Above: Every house has its own well and somelike the one shown here, have hand-pumps to bring the water up to the surface. Photograph: H.U. Khan.

Right: A typical street in the commune — the streets are collectively kept clean and neat. Photograph: H.U. Khan.

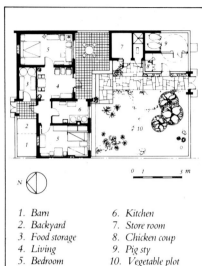

1. Barn
2. Backyard
3. Food storage
4. Living
5. Bedroom
6. Kitchen
7. Store room
8. Chicken coup
9. Pig sty
10. Vegetable plot

Above and above right: Plan and sketch of winning entry, 1981 Rural Housing Competition in China, by Chu Pi Cheng and Liu Song Tow, Tian Jin. Courtesy of Architectural Journal No. 10 1981.
Right: In the Muslim quarter around the Xi'an Great Mosque, the street is bounded by inward-looking houses. Photograph: P. Clement.
Right below: Plan of a typical urban courtyard house, near the Xi'an Great Mosque. Drawing: H.U. Khan.
Far below: The highrise flats lining the city streets have been nicknamed "the wall of shame" by local inhabitants. Photograph: B. Taylor.

spaces, grouping of volumes or in actual execution. Villages are the norm, and the dwelling is an integral part of a complex. Thus, the observer's eye is attracted by the alignment of walls, the groups of houses, the repetition of doorways following a certain rhythm, the quality of detailing on doors, the form and elegance of roof lines. In these rural areas, such characteristics have nothing to do with a nostalgic yearning for the past; on the contrary, they represent traditions that are very much alive. They illustrate the permanence of a certain traditional expertise concerning formal typologies and constructive techniques perfected over centuries.

This fact seems extremely positive, and one which the public authorities ought to meditate upon at a time when they have just sponsored for the first time a vast competition dealing with the rural habitat. The results of this national competition for rural housing were published[1] in October, 1981: out of 6500 projects entered, 142 were given recognition and will be widely disseminated throughout the whole country. Let us hope that those who are taking up the problem, the architects, the building contractors and regional planning groups, will consider and respect the good qualities of existing housing and traditional know-how, particularly the simplest techniques and uses of material

[1]Jianzhu Xuebao, Architectural Journal, China No. 10, 1981.

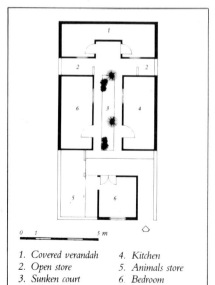

1. Covered verandah
2. Open store
3. Sunken court
4. Kitchen
5. Animals store
6. Bedroom

Rural House near Turfan

In the village, this is the house of a middle income family. The mud house is designed on three levels with the lowest as entrance and store; the middle level for animals and the family living spaces on the top.

Right: The main family living area on the top floor is shaded by vines. This open space is used for sleeping, meeting guests and cooking. In winter the family members sleep indoors. Photograph: H.U. Khan.

Below: The ground floor entrance to the house, viewed from the inside — the approach to the dwelling is also covered with vines. Photograph: C. Little.

Below right: Detail of the balcony and cooking area showing the pot storage areas and earth chimney. Photograph: P. Clement.

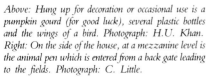

Above: Hung up for decoration or occasional use is a pumpkin gourd (for good luck), several plastic bottles and the wings of a bird. Photograph: H.U. Khan.

Right: On the side of the house, at a mezzanine level is the animal pen which is entered from a back gate leading to the fields. Photograph: C. Little.

which rural people still handle so well. This was the basic message of Professor Liu Dunzhen in his book on the Chinese house.[1]

The organisation of living spaces merits our special attention. As we noted earlier, the essential aspect of a Chinese dwelling is that of an enclosure delineated by walls, an interior space, and a centre. These three elements are found at different scales, according to the natural environment of the surrounding area: the five sacred mountains, four in each of the directions of the compass and one in the centre; or in a political framework of space: a region and its centre, the capital.[2] The same concern for enclosure is to be found in the city: "Walls, walls, and yet walls, form the framework of every Chinese city", says Siren, and "the Chinese used the same word *Cheng* for a

city and a city wall ... there is no real city in China without a surrounding wall.[3] But today the walls which encircled Beijing have been torn down and replaced by large avenues, where armies of bicyclists confront a few automobiles, and the same avenues are lined with huge complexes of apartment buildings so disliked by the population that they have been nicknamed "the wall of shame"!

Walls are found not only around each community, small city, village or neighbourhood inhabited by Han Chinese, but also in Central Asia where the nomads encircle their camps with earth ramparts. Walls and ramparts of earth occur everywhere from Beijing to Kashi, giving dwellings the look of fortresses.

It is necessary to note this Chinese way of thinking about space in order to analyse the plan of the house and its development towards an ideal model that is closed on four sides around an inner courtyard. Once the ideal has been attained, extension is carried out by multiplication of the ele-

In Kashi, the bright colours of people's clothes contrast strikingly with the earth houses and green fields. Photograph: C. Little.

ments, whether it is a large residence or grouping in a neighbourhood.

The enclosing wall is penetrated by a single door to the exterior, usually oriented to the south, while the other walls remain free for other blocks to be attached. This doorway, which is truly a filter, is usually decorated, even if it was once linked to a need for protection against evil influences or energies.

The central courtyard of dwellings, expanded in size in rural areas to allow for agricultural activities and livestock, can also be found in cities extremely reduced in size because of the narrowness of lots bordered by party walls on either side. This is the case for houses in Xi'an, where one enters by a lateral corridor; the space for circulation is narrow at the front of the house and becomes larger towards the rear, as one moves from the street towards the principal living quarters at the far end of the courtyard. The corridor leads us into a narrow first courtyard where there are two rooms; the passage way then becomes narrower

[1]*Liu Dunzhen, Zhongguo Zhuzhai Gaishuo, translated into French as La maison chinoise — Paris: 1980, Ed. Berger Levrault (Reviewed in this issue — editors).*

[2]*Le pays lui-même ne s'appelle déjà t-il pas Zhongguo "L'Empire du milieu"; sur cette notion appliquée à la ville voir Paul Wheatley, The Pivot of the Four Quarters, Edinburgh University Press, 1971.*

[3]*Cited by J. Needham, Science and Civilisation in China Vol. IV, No. 3. Cambridge University Press, 1971, p. 42.*

Urban House in Turfan

This village house is not really 'urban' as it is one of the smaller village settlements near the town. It does however display the character of an urban dwelling in its two-storey and closely-packed buildings.

Top: The house from its internal courtyard. The eldest son and his family live in the rooms above. The lower rooms are used for storage. Photograph: H.U. Khan.
Below: Stairs leading to the son's quarters. Photograph: H.U. Khan.
Top right: The kitchen-dining area. Note the calendar on the wall showing Muslim monuments. Photograph: B. Taylor.
Right: The living room-bedroom of the house. The food has been prepared for visitors. Photograph: B. Taylor.
Below right: The son's room. The bedding is stacked during the day. Photograph: C. Little.

between two lateral arrangements of rooms and ultimately comes to the main part of the house. Urban dwellings in Xi'an can be richly decorated with sculpted wood and latticework, as was visible in houses around the Great Mosque in Xi'an.

Compared to the classical severity of houses with wings disposed around a courtyard, or with the elegant grayness of brick walls and tiled roofs of Beijing's old quarters, the rural dwellings possess considerable typological variety, characterised by their different relationships with the earth, as a basic support and as a building material. Thus, on the loess plateau alone of Shaanxi we discovered completely subterranean houses in pits or caves, detached houses above ground and totally unexpected intermediary solutions. The terracing of these loess canyons, natural or manmade, often allows one to enter either from the level below, or, in other cases, by long sunken ramps that descend into the court.

While earth is still the material most frequently used in Xinjiang, it is in the form of sun-dried bricks or adobe. Once the bricks have been laid to form a wall, they are covered with a mud coating in such a way that the house and even the village seems to be a fortress blending into the landscape. The old necessity for defence is still a factor in the choice of sites and Kashi still provides a living example of this.

The interior arrangement of the dwelling enclosure has an almost Mediterranean aspect. The Uygur house, whose building materials are more malleable, contrasts sharply with the crispness and severity of angles and forms of han structures, whether in cities or the countryside: the former have softer, rounder angles and more flowing, rather than jagged forms. The houses in Shaanxi, like those all across the loess plateau, take into account the extremes of temperature, especially hot summers by digging into the earth, forming courtyards at the bottom of the pit which remain shaded and cool, whereas in Xinjiang, interiors extend outwards onto roof terraces covered with trellises. Flat roofs and terraces made with earth contrast here with the steeply pitched roofs of Shaanxi where, like Roman impluvium, rainwater runs off into the courtyard and is recovered by an underground cistern.

Wood is rare in Xinjiang, and apart from small, round tree-trunks set across adobe walls and then covered, one sees practically no wood framing. Occasionally, rooms are covered by barrel vaults made of sun-dried bricks. Whatever timber is used is grown in the oasis itself, mainly poplars, which line the roadsides and later serve to support the terraces.

From the point of view of building, there is a clear delineation between the two

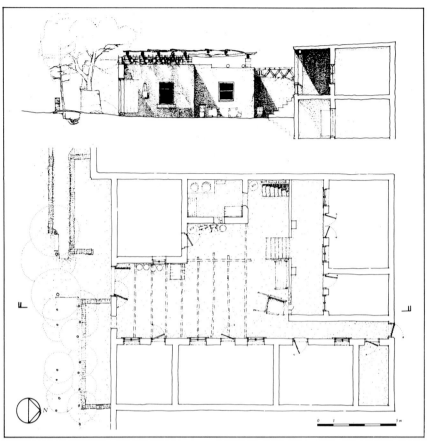

worlds: on the one hand, the wooden skeletal structure with infill which can generally be found across the Far East and South Asia, and on the other, load-bearing wall construction. In Central Asia there are few wooden supports, aside from those sculptured or painted on verandahs or prestigious buildings such as mosques: elsewhere thick bearing walls are the rule, carrying vaults, cupolas and terraces. In this respect the area reminds one of Afghanistan, Iran, and even certain areas of North Africa.

Regions of Han civilisation possess framed houses that have pitched roofs supported by wood skeletons, while the walls are simply screens. This kind of construction, which requires careful preparation and assembling, and the use of metal tools for cutting and shaping elements, distributes the forces onto lightweight structure. Such a system follows laws radically different from those governing mud brick construction based upon forces in compression.

In Xinjiang numerous details catch the eye. Doorways are still very often composed of a circle inscribed in a square. Screens of mud brick or timber *mushrabiya* separate interior spaces from the exterior. The edges of terraces are decorated, and incorporate benches and outdoor fireplaces. Open galleries on an upper floor, trellises in front of houses and gardens behind are all aspects of a seasonal occupation of various dwelling spaces. Large earthen walls form-

Plan and section of a house in Turfan. Drawings courtesy of T. Chastain, R. Chow and P. Hajiaw, associated with the Aga Khan Programmes for Islamic Architecture at M.I.T.; from a forthcoming article on settlement and dwelling forms.

ing animal pens are located independently of the houses at suitable points in a village.

A certain harmony in colour that of the earth of house and landscape, prevails in the environment. This makes all the more remarkable the vivid colours of Uygur dress and ornamentation. Such bright colouring is also applied to some architectural elements: columns, shutters, door and window frames, railings; and is found on furniture and on decorative objects such as cupboards, cradles, rugs and fabrics. In the depths of the main living room in a house, above a niche which used to be reserved for religious images, can be found two red stars: one of them in relief, the other flat, mounted on an embroidered curtain and surrounded by other engravings.

The Uygur town also provides an interest which contrasts with the gray tiles and walls of Beijing or Xi'an, with their rigidly orthogonal streets. Kashi has streets whose organic quality stems from their adaptation to a rugged site and supple lines of local architecture. Cubical blocks of earth sheltering spaces for habitation and overlooking courtyards and streets, create an urban landscape that calls to mind the distant pueblos of New Mexico.

Left: The fortified town of Kashi (just sixty miles from the USSR and Pakistani borders), on the Silk Route is still generally out of bounds to foreigners. Photograph: C. Little.

Left, below: Houses in Kashi are on a multitude of levels, connected by an intricate network of pedestrian streets. Photograph: C. Little.

Pierre Clément is a French architect involved in research at the Institut Français d'Architecture in Paris. He edits a series entitled 'Architectures' and his publications include 'La Maison Chinoise' 1979.

Underground Houses

C H I N A

The 'Loess Region' of China contains firm hard-packed soil out of which the inhabitants have carved their courtyard homes.

They are generally located along the southern bank of the Yellow River and on the Northwest Plateau. Loess, also known as *Huangtu* (Yellow Earth), is a fine loamy silt or clay blown and packed by wind. Loess began to be deposited sometime during the last Ice Age. Strong winds from the steppes of Asia brought fine dust southwards and spread it out, mainly in the provinces of Shaanxi, Henan, Gansu, and southern

a steep expanse of thick Loess is exposed, such as alongside a gully, it is easy to dig into the surface and construct living quarters.

The existence of these cave dwellings is recorded in the writings of the Western Zhou Dynasty (11th century to 771 B.C.) and the Eastern Han Dynasty (25 — 220 A.D.). Frequently mentioned are sunken courtyards, an excellent winter shelter, as the Loess formation provides exceptionally efficient natural insulation from the cold. At the same time, the thick walls and ceilings provide an "air-conditioned" coolness during the hot summer months.

The utilisation of this Loess soil for

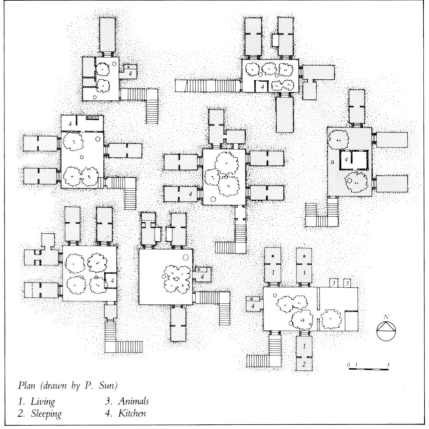

Plan (drawn by P. Sun)

1. Living
2. Sleeping
3. Animals
4. Kitchen

Above: Family units in the West Village near Kunghsin, Henan.
Right: Vaulted and strongly defined entrance to an underground room. Photograph: C. Little.
Far right: A typical pit dwelling in Shaanxi province. Photograph: J. Oubo.

Hingxia, and covered an area of 631,000 square kilometres, or approximately 6.6 per cent of the whole territory of China. The deposits can be as much as 80 metres in thickness. The land form in this region appears mainly as a high table-like plain with abruptly descending edges, with gorges and gullies at various locations. As a consequence, the cave or pit dwelling is a distinctive form in this region, where the Loess is thick and timber is scarce. These dwellings require little timber, for wherever

Text and drawings by Paul Sun

construction has also resulted in surprisingly pleasant courtyards as well as cleverly arranged subterranean villages, such as the West Village near Kunghsien, Henan, a village of approximately 5,000 people that dates back to the Sui Dynasty (561 — 618 A.D.). The village is surrounded by a wall approximately 6 to 8 metres high of Loess soil on three sides and is bounded by a Loess gully on one side. The majority of the dwellings are subterranean, with sunken courtyards.

On entering the typical village gate, one first sees only treetops protruding from the courtyards. The typical sunken courtyard is about 15 by 15 metres, and is approximately 10 metres below the natural grade. An L-shaped or U-shaped stairway leads down to the courtyard through a simple entry gateway at the courtyard level. The living and sleeping chambers are excavated on all sides. The basic layout is traditional, with all major living spaces facing south for exposure to the sun and organised in an inward and axial plan. The courtyard, like all typical courtyard houses throughout China, allows sunlight into the inner spaces and provides an outdoor activity space: a place for the unity of the family. For the majority of the Chinese population, the extended family still survives. The ideal has been for the family to live together in a large house with many generations under one roof. The actual physical limitations including the confinement of these sunken courtyards have continued to hold the family together, even during the Cultural Revolution's de-emphasis of family clans.

The interiors of the underground cave chambers are vaulted, 3 metres in height, 3 metres in width, and generally 6 to 8 metres deep. The chambers are often divided into two parts by a masonry storage bin. The outer portion serves as living space and is usually lined with brick and sometimes has a recessed niche for sitting or sleeping and there are large windows and doorways which provide natural light. The inner area is primarily for sleeping or storage. Sometimes the chambers are two stories high, with a loft for sleeping.

Located in the semi-arid region of China, where the temperature in the winter months is usually below freezing, annual precipitation averages 250-500 millimetres, and evaporation is over 1,000 millimetres per year: the subterranean dwelling is ideally suited for this climate. Earth is an excellent insulation because it has the capacity for moderating temperature. There is no need for central heating for the caves except for the traditional *Kang* (heated masonry bed) and certainly no need for cooling during the summer. The living chamber and the courtyard areas are ventilated by suction: negative air pressure in the courtyard is created by a strong wind sweeping over the plateaux circulating the air by literally sucking it out of the ground. A well dug in the courtyard can drain surface water, and because of generally light rainfall, prevents the danger of Loess landslide or collapse.

Historically, these subterranean dwellings have served as more than homes. During World War II they were used as shelters for soldiers and storage places for both food and ammunition. Those villages with underground tunnels connecting the sunken courtyards played a significant part in the successful guerilla war against the Japanese invaders.

There are also sunken courtyards with partial cave dwellings and partial houses in the courts. The houses are well protected from winter winds and provide a choice of living areas for the family.

In certain regions, there are cuts through the hillsides that form streets with cave dwellings on either side. A small, walled front court with an entrance gateway leads to the courtyards beyond. The courtyards are shaded by fruit trees and broad-leafed trees. The trees lining the street also give the impression of an above-ground dwelling rather than one that is in the ground. This form of architecture does not apply only to residential areas. There are also office spaces, schools and hotels which occupy a series of sunken courtyards or are dug into the hillsides.

For centuries, the Chinese have learned to live with the land. The Great Wall was built on top of the highest ridges of mountains to provide vantage points. The tiered rice fields of Sichnan ensure that all cultivatable land is utilised. The natural landscape along the Yangtze River has remained unspoiled, exemplifying the traditional Chinese understanding that man should harmonise with nature rather than dominate it. Dwellings in the Loess plateau, though conforming to a basic floor plan, climate and available resources, require regional variations. They utilise natural resources to provide shelter that is hardly in need of any "utilities" as we know them.

As we become increasingly energy conscious, we can learn from the earth sheltered architecture conceived by those ancient anonymous builders whose concepts indicate imaginative solutions to our present-day environmental problems. Though modern technology contributes to the changing rural scene in China, at the same time it threatens local traditions of architectural landscaping. The Chinese are struggling with the temptation of standardising architectural design and adapting western design concepts while maintaining their traditional values. Dwellings in the Loess plateau provide the best case for maintaining traditional values.

As we face resource depletion, it appears to be time to reconsider what the earth itself has to offer. This is not to say we should build cave dwellings, but rather utilise the earth's natural thermal qualities in conjunction with the application of modern technology — electricity, materials for interior finishes, proper water supply and sewage systems, etc. The subterranean courtyard houses could be ideal for new communities of the future.

Right, top: The cave dwellings are serviced by a road bevelled on the hillside near Xi'an. Photograph: H.U. Khan.

Right, below: The interior court of a typical dwelling is surrounded by rooms (caves) on three sides whilst a wall screening the house from the road forms the fourth side. Photograph: H.U. Khan.

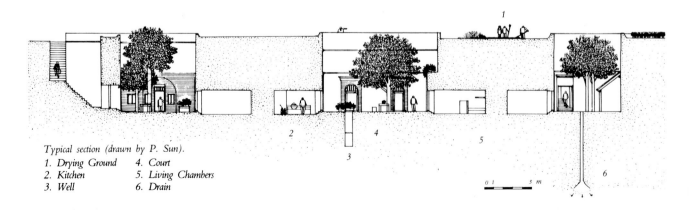

Typical section (drawn by P. Sun).
1. Drying Ground   4. Court
2. Kitchen   5. Living Chambers
3. Well   6. Drain

*Paul Sun was a Chinese-American architect,
partner in the firm Shepley, Bullfinch, Richardson
and Abbot in Boston, U.S.A. He was also a
visiting lecturer in many Chinese universities. Mr
Sun unfortunately died in 1986.*

The DUTCH COLONIAL VILLA

INDONESIA

Text and photographs by
Helen Jessup.

A picture of the typical Dutch Indies house emerges from literary sources as thick-walled, high-ceilinged and marble- or tile-floored, with a large central room giving onto a deep verandah in front and back. Sleeping-rooms open off the central room on both sides of this central room, and these sometimes also open onto the frequently occurring narrower side gallery which gives access to the rear without disturbing the main room. Cooking and bathing facilities, as well as storerooms and servants' quarters, are at the rear in subsidiary buildings often linked to the main structure by covered walkways. Sometimes there are separate pavilions for guest quarters. All are set in large grounds with lush planting, a circular driveway sweeping past imposing front steps, or an avenue of Royal palms leading majestically to the entrance.

This image has so dominated the conception of the Netherlands presence in what is now Indonesia that the style has come to be known as 'Dutch Colonial'. 'Dutch-Indies' and hence 'colonial' it may be, but truly 'Dutch' it is not. Even a fleeting visit to any major Netherlands city unchanged by the devastation of the Second World War leaves an entirely different impression. Homogeneous in profile, height and building-line, multi-storeyed, attached and generously fenestrated, the gabled brick houses in such towns as Amsterdam, Haarlem and Delft harmonise to create the rational, calm, intensely urban

Above: Row of houses in Plantagemiddenlaan, Amsterdam, showing typical gables, homogeneity of height and profile of Netherlands urban architecture. The centre house is rather unusual in having pilasters flanking the central window on the top storey and columns supporting a small third floor balcony. Below: Photograph, probably taken at the turn of the century, showing avenue of Royal palms leading to a neoclassical colonial villa in Jakarta. The house is now dilapidated and altered.

townscape so unmistakably Dutch. Classical proportion between house rows, canals and bridges links the centuries and the cities in a common heritage. Netherlands towns show relatively few traces of the Classical Revival which swept northern European cities in the nineteenth century and determined

much of the present appearance of, for example, London and Paris.

Why then did the colonising Dutch in the Indies build in a idiom so completely different from that of their homeland, a style which has nevertheless come to be named after them? An examination of many of the remaining buildings constructed by the Dutch in Indonesia before the middle of the nineteenth century, and of early engravings and drawings illustrating old Dutch Indies structures, reveals that for over two hundred years they did not in fact build in the 'Dutch Colonial' style. Early fort buildings are heavy, four-square; early churches would fit comfortably into a traditional Dutch landscape painting. The 1707 Stadhuis of Batavia, now the Jakarta Historical Museum, without deep eaves, balconies or verandahs, makes no tropical concessions and reminds the visitor more of the old Town Hall in Amsterdam than of the conventional image of Indies architecture.

Nor does the 1760 National Archives building, formerly the house of Reinier de Klerk, a governor of the VOC, as the Vereenigde Oostindische Campagnie, or United East Indian Company, is usually called. The comfortable symmetry of this solid building with its flanking gabled pavilions springs from a Dutch bourgeois tradition having little in common with the colonnaded 'Dutch Colonial' house of literature and tradition.

The 1768 description by Stavorinus, a sea captain in the service of the VOC, of the Dutch houses of his time in Batavia calls to mind the so-called *Toko Merah* (red shop) still standing in the old part of Jakarta. It is a double house of the mid-eighteenth century, severe, two-storeyed, with dark red tiled floors and red painted interior woodwork. Most houses of this period were strongly shuttered, not only against intruders but against the air as well, and they lacked any special architectural modifications to protect the occupants from fierce sun or torrential tropical rain. Sometimes the houses had a small inner courtyard, so their functions devolved inwards in direct constrast to the 'Dutch Colonial' villa, where household activities spilled outward at front and rear. Inventories for a Semarang house dated 1809 list rotan panels for the windows; glass was apparently unknown before the brief period of British rule under Raffles between 1811 and 1816. Gardens were few because of the scarcity of land within the

Top: The Toko Merah, *Jakarta, of about 1730. This double house is a further example of the early closed style of Dutch houses in the Indies.*
Above: The Gedung Pancasila, *formerly the house of the Saxe-Weimar family and later the seat of the Volksraad, of about 1830. Its simple neoclassical form is typical of the best of the domestic formal style. It was in this building, behind which the high-rise building of the Foreign Ministry rises, that the late President Sukarno made his speech about the doctrine of Pancasila whose five principles are integral to the Indonesian national creed.*

towns, which in the early centuries had been walled for security reasons. Health conditions were appalling and the mortality rate among both Dutch and indigenous residents was high.

When and why did the Dutch Indies house change so radically? Neither question is easy to answer precisely, but the timing is certainly linked to the emergence of the Indies as an official colony of the Netherlands government. This came about only after the dissolution of the bankrupt VOC in 1798–99, at which time the Netherlands government was itself under French hegemony. For health reasons the first Governor-General, General H.W. Daendels, moved the administrative centre from overcrowded Batavia on its marshy coastal site to a contiguous area further south, which was named Weltevreden. With the increased security and stability arising from the more committed official government, the town could expand beyond its previous walled confines. With more available land, gardens and broader streets were possible, and the

physical conditions then existed for a change in domestic architecture within the city. Less restricted types of house had previously been built on country estates, which will be discussed later, but it is probable that the first real 'Dutch Colonial' types appeared not long after the restoration of Dutch authority following the defeat of the French in Europe and the subsequent withdrawal of the British from Java in 1816.

A fairly early example of the changed type still in good condition is the 1830's *Gedung Pancasila* (Pancasila building), formerly the house of a member of the noble Saxe-Weimar family and later the site of the Volksraad (People's Council). Eight Doric columns stand imposingly across the front of its simple porch, which is flush with the ground rather than commandingly atop a flight of steps. Behind the porch floor-length windows flank the central door. The proportions are noble but unpretentious, grand but not grandiose. Old pictures of the house give us a better idea of its presence than we can hope for today, when a necessary but clumsy administrative extension building towers over it.

Although this type proliferated in the nineteenth century, not every Dutch Indies house achieved the elegance of the *Gedung Pancasila*. In 1870 the Dutch literary critic and historian Conrad Busken Huet declared in a letter to a friend in the Netherlands that to create a Batavian villa one needed only to brush with whitewash a Zealand cowshed with its long, drooping roof, and add some thick pillars. He described the roof of an Indies house as a playground for rats in the dry season and a sieve through which the rain trickled onto furniture and books during the wet season. Batavian houses, he claimed, had bad proportions and impossible lines. They nevertheless became more refined as the century progressed until even middle-level Dutch officials could expect to live in a house resembling the one remembered by Dermoût's Riek.

One can only surmise the reasons for the change in domestic architecture. One cause can possibly be found in the expanding role of the colonial government. As the interests of the Netherlands inhabitants of the Indies developed beyond the earlier mere trading concerns, as the numbers of Netherlanders who came to stay on a more permanent basis increased, as the importance of the colony to the Netherlands economy expanded, so the civil infrastructure burgeoned. Not just trading interests but the administration, development and well-being of the entire country and its indigenous and foreign population alike had to be taken care of. This implied a direct involvement with the Indonesian people and their culture in a manner quite different from the practice of VOC times.

In such conditions, where a central colonial government unified the Indies in a way not known before (even though it was not until the twentieth century that the Dutch succeeded in controlling the whole archipelago), it would have been natural to try to express in a tangible way the presence and power of the colonisers. A look at the conquerors of recent centuries reveals the British as the most notable examples. Drawing as they did on Greek and Roman precedent to enhance their imperial philosophy, they invoked the nobility implicit in the architecture of these ancient powers and gave impetus to the nineteenth-century Neoclassical Revival. The grand style was applied not only in the cities of Britain itself but also in their colonies in Africa, Asia, America and Australia. Imposing buildings like the Mint in Calcutta and the Secretariat building in Pretoria are clearly more satisfactory expressions of imperial might than the models the Dutch were offered by the restrained bourgeois elegance of their own architecture.

It is not unreasonable to explain on this basis the Dutch choice of uncharacteristic neoclassical form for such Batavian buildings as the *Gedung Bicara* (the former Justice Building, now the Museum *Seni Rupa*, or Fine Arts Museum) of about 1870. It can also explain the Museum of the Batavia Society for Arts and Sciences (incidentally the oldest society of its kind in Asia) of 1862–68, now the Museum *Pusat*, or Central Museum, and the *Istana Merdeka* (Freedom Palace) of 1873–79, among others. Examples of neoclassical style can be found as well in other Indonesian cities where the Dutch had an established presence before the end of the nineteenth century, such as the Governor's Residence of 1870 in Surabaya and the *Balai Kota* (Town Hall) of about the same time in Semarang.

The need for visible proof of an imperial presence may account for the adoption of neoclassical style for public buildings, but it cannot adequately ex-

Top: The Museum Seni Rupa *(Fine Arts Museum), the so-called* Gedung Bicara, *or Justice building, of about 1870 is one of the most dignified of Jakarta's neoclassical public buildings.*
Above: The colonnaded front verandah of the building also shown in Figure 1 reveals the importance of this area in the way of life of Dutch Indies families before the twentieth century.

plain the great number of other examples, particularly the 'Dutch Colonial' houses already described. True, these are colonnaded in a manner similar to the neoclassical models, and true, the verandah columns are often in classical mould.

What makes them different, apart from the fact that they often lack a fully-developed classical pediment or cornice, is largely a matter of scale and atmosphere. Whereas the impression created by the columns in the *Gedung Bicara*, for instance, is of loftiness and dignity, the columns shown in photographs of a now dilapidated nineteenth century house of the 'Dutch Colonial' type in the outskirts of the old city of Jakarta seem rather to offer domesticated privacy. The colonnaded space in the former is public, noble; in the latter, intimate and secluded.

8

7

There are still some houses of this type which have neither been neglected nor converted to public buildings. One notable example is to be found in Pasuruan, East Java, in the house belonging to the Tjoa family. In this region grand houses abound, witness to the wealth formerly generated by prosperous sugar plantations, but few have been maintained in the excellent condition of this one. The front verandah is dignified without being pompous, while the rear verandah has the relaxed elegance of a well-to-do family life like the one we infer from the photographs of the Jakarta house mentioned above and also from Sumatran plantation residences as depicted in albums from around the turn of the century.

9

Adaptation to the tropical climate offers a simple explanation of the development of high ceilings, low-sweeping roofs and wide verandahs in these 'Dutch Colonial' houses. Certainly these features, helping to mitigate sun and rain, must have played an important part in the success and popularity of the style, but like the imperial visibility theory they do not fully account for the stylistic details. Another cause can perhaps be discovered by considering a few houses outside Jakarta which were referred to earlier. Dilapidated, often extensively altered, they are remnants of former country estates which predate the official colony and conscious neoclassicism and which differ from it in several respects. Climatic concessions alone provide no more convincing a genesis for these buildings than for later imperial types. A good example, the house known as the 'Japan' house, dates from the second half of the eighteenth century. Its roof sweeps from a steeper central section in a long gentle line to form broad verandahs supported by columns much slenderer than typical neoclassical examples. The lines of these houses, although formal and symmetrical, are simpler and more graceful than those of many later neoclassical types; the roof lines are gentler and they look more at home in their tropical setting.

To find a convincing source for this kind of house one should look not only at climatic and European influences but also at indigenous architecture. The earliest images of this can be seen in many of the bas reliefs on the eighth century Buddhist temple of Borobudur and the ninth century temple complex of Loro Jonggrang at Prambanan, both in Central Java. In the carvings one frequently glimpses groups of people sitting in small pillared structures, some of which appear grand, while others are clearly domestic in scale and atmosphere.

The small pavilions depicted often have multi-layered roofs, which are supported by several types of column. Sometimes they are raised on platforms and sometimes are at ground level. The basic construction principles are convincingly posited by the Dutch architect Henri Maclaine Pont (in *Javanese Architecture* of 1923–24) as direct antecedents of *kraton* (palace) architecture in a continuous tradition beginning in the Hindu-Javanese temples and palaces of

Top: A Medan, Sumatra, house of the nineteenth century. This 1890's photograph reveals that the verandah played an important part in provincial life as well as in the more central areas of Java.

Above: Part of a bas relief frieze on the temple of Borobudur showing a group of people sitting in a pendopo-like pavilion.

Below: One of the noblest pendopos of all, the Pendopo Agung of 1810, in the Mangkunegaran kraton in Solo, Central Java.

Central Java, surviving in the East Java temples from the twelfth to the fifteenth centuries, and still existing in the modern *kratons* of Yogyakarta, Solo and Cirebon.

Of the structures traditionally found in *kraton* complexes, it is the pillared *pendopo* used for formal social gatherings which suggests the closest functional as well as stylistic precedent for the 'Dutch Colonial' gallery, or front verandah. One can also find indigenous buildings which bridge the social and scale differences between the palatial and the domestic. The *panggerangans* of regional administrators (the district *bupatis*) with their deep low verandahs, where unpretentious poles support broad roofs in simple dignity, are a direct link between the *kraton pendopo* and the colonial villa. It is probably not accidental that the emergence of this colonial style coincided with the greater involvement of the Dutch with indigenous society after the beginning of the colony proper in the nineteenth century as well as with the growing consciousness of that need to express the rulers' power which turned to classical models.

One of the oldest examples of a colonial structure adapting the characteristics of indigenous form to European use can be seen in the now shabby early eighteenth century house which was formerly the residence of the governor of Tidore in North Maluku. The European columns framing the shallow porch link it with later neoclassical types, but the porch itself and the vernacular profile and material of the *atap* (palm thatch) roof are more reminiscent of *kampung* (village) houses. On the nearby island of Ternate, the Sultan's palace offers a similar combination of indigenous and western features. The stilts raising it above ground level derive directly from Bugis, Minahasa and Maluku vernacular precedents, whereas its verandahs have been bowed and railed, which lends them the air of balconies of a distinctly European kind.

It is not only among noble structures that one finds precedents for the colonnaded verandah. Not just the porches of houses in Javanese *desas* (rural villages) but also the balcony-like front sections of the stilted houses of Sulawesi give vernacular variants of the form. So do the raised 'streets' running the length of the Dayak longhouses of Kalimantan, where many of the domestic and social events of the village take place.

Above: A bupati's *residence, the* Panggerangan Aria Gandasubrata, in Banyumas, Central Java, showing the colonnaded front verandah so similar to the neoclassical versions yet also close to the simple desa houses to be found in many parts of Java.*

Below: Former Governor's residence, Tidore, N. Maluku, showing combination of vernacular roof-line and material with European columns.
Bottom: Minahasa, N. Sulawesi, house on stilts showing balcony-like area in front which serves the same purpose as the porch in Java.

By the wide geographic occurrence and multiple application of this form, one is convinced of its pervasiveness; indigenous architecture throughout Indonesia typically provides a covered but open area linking inner closed space with the outdoors. A notable non-domestic application of this principle can be found in the characteristic Javanese mosque. The verandah-like *surambi* situated in front of the mosque's principal chamber is not only an area for prayer at times when the inner area is filled, but also serves as a place for the teaching and social functions of the mosque. Like the small waiting-*pendopos* at the Kesepuhan *kraton* in Cirebon, the *surambi* has a dignified but friendly atmosphere. The scale is human, even when the area is as large as at the *Mesjid Agung* (Great Mosque) in Demak, in contrast to the soaring spaces with their immense columns in the mosque's interior.

The climatic and cultural suitability of this form was probably a factor in the evolution of the Dutch Indies house, but one can find another application of it in school and hospital architecture. Adequate air circulation is achieved by a layout where wings and separate pavilions are linked by colonnaded 'corridors'.

Not every example of the colonnaded precinct fits into the preceding categories. For example, one can point to the charming urban *kampung* of Wuwutan in Surabaya. Here one feels the vernacular has borrowed from the colonial. The amusingly disproportionate neoclassical columns have been adopted neither for structural support nor social symbol but for stylistic fantasy alone.

Why did the Dutch abandon the neoclassical-indigenous amalgam as a model for domestic architecture around the beginning of the twentieth century? There were many probable causes, important among which were doubtless the growing scarcity and value of land and the rising cost of labour and materials which followed the rapid growth of the Dutch population of the Indies at that time. Another cause may be traceable to the changing nature of the coloniser, who began to look on the Indies in those years not as a remote and exotic land but almost as an extension of the Netherlands. Such a settler, destined to remain in the colony for long periods of time or even for an entire career, and having an established family with him, was unlike

Top: Small pendopos *in front of the main buildings of the Kesepuhan* kraton *in Cirebon, W. Java. These pavilions are clearly descendants of the types shown in early bas reliefs like those in Figure 11.*
Above: An eclectic use of neoclassical columns for the minimal verandahs of kampung *houses in Wuwutan, Surabaya.*

earlier Netherlanders, typically bachelors, who usually stayed only long enough to amass a fortune or fulfil a contract. The new resident was more likely to demand housing emphasising the connected, Dutch nature of the colony. Yet another explanation may lie in the evolution, particularly after the First World War, of the idea that the Indies had to play a role in the modern world, in which case an international architectural idiom would have been seen as more appropriate than

in indigenous or regional one.

Much of the domestic architecture of the Netherlands Indies between 1900 and 1942, with some notable exceptions attributable to the talents of a few outstanding architects, therefore developed along the lines of surburban European models. Sometimes this was modified by planting, so that the basic structure was all but enveloped in tropical growth, but for the most part the houses offered neither charm, stylistic distinction nor climatic appropriateness. Nor are current trends encouraging. The recent urge to 'modernise' has led to the total destruction or the modification of older houses, so that lacy fretwork on porches and roof gables, for example, has been replaced in many places by heavy fascias, and the window hoods and verandahs which formerly kept off rain and sun

A typical example of the unimaginative borrowing of suburban European architecture for middle-class housing in the 1920's. Furnished with no balconies or rain-hoods, these houses lack protection from sun and rain are often airless and hot.

have been sheared off leaving houses resembling eyes without eyelids. More alarming still, *kampung* houses which once had walls of *gedek* (split woven bamboo), cheap and airy despite its limited life, are being replaced by multi-family buildings in unmodified western style, often of concrete. Lacking roof drainage and eave protection, this material rapidly mildews in the hot and humid climate, so that the dwellings are not only uncomfortably airless but also depressingly stained. The effect of unattractive and uncomfortable surroundings on the morale of a society is well documented.

In the 1920's and 1930's the work and writings of a few enlightened architects and town planners such as Henri Maclaine Pont, Thomas Karsten, Soerjo Winoto and Notodiningrat urged the careful study and conservation of indigenous architecture for the sake of cultural continuity and social and stylistic integrity as well as climatic suitability. It is still not too late to keep their advice and example in mind and to preserve the architectural heritage of Indonesia, predominantly indigenous but after three and a half centuries of Dutch presence also inevitably partly European; but time is running out.

Bibliography

Bosboom, H.D.H.
Oude woningen in de stad Batavia; Den Haag, 1898.

Couperus, Louis
The Hidden Force, translated by Alexander Teixeira de Mattos; Londong, 1922.

Dermout, Maria
The Ten Thousand Things, translated by Hans Koningsberger; New York, 1958.

Dermout, Maria
Yesterday, translated by Hans Koningsberger; New York, 1959.

Kalff, S.
'Europeesche huizen te Batavia', *Nederlandsh-Indië Oud en Nieuw*, Vol II, 1971–18, pp 77–91.

Kemp, P.H. van der
'Over kunst in Indische woningbouw', *Nederlandsch-Indische Huis Oud en Nieuw*, Vol II, No. 2, 1915, pp 1–7.

Maclaine Pont, Henri
'Javaansche Architectuur', *Djawa*, 1923 No's 3 & 4, 1924 No. 1.

Nieuwenhuys, Rob
In de Schommelstoel, een keuze uit de Indisch-Nederlandse letterkunde van 1870 tot 1935; Amsterdam, 1975.

Nieuwenhuys, Rob
Mirror of the Indies, translated by Frans van Rosevelt, edited by E.M. Beekman, Amherst, 1982.

Nijs, E. Breton de
Faded Portraits, translated by Donald and Elsie Sturtevant; Amherst, 1983.

Stavorinus, Johan S.
'Voyages to the East Indies', *Insulinde*, Edited by Corneia Niekus Moore, Hawaii, 1978.

Steinmetz, C.
'Oude Hollandsche buitenplaatsen van Batavia', *Cultureel Indië VII*, (no date available), pp 171–181.

Wall, V.J. van der
'Oude Hollandsche Bouwkunst in Indonesiä, *Hollandsche koloniale bouwkunst in de XVII° en XVIII° eeuw*; Antwerp, 1942.

Winoto, Soerjo
'De Regentswoning', *Nederlandsch-Indië Oud en Nieuw*, Vol. IV, No. 5, 1919, pp 130–148.

Helen Jessup has spent many years in Indonesia. She has written several articles on colonial architecture in Indonesia and has travelled widely researching this subject. She is presently working on her doctorate.

The MALAY HOUSE

'The Malay House' has been specially written
for MIMAR by Professor Wardi, who until recently was
Dean of the School of Architecture
at the Universiti Technologi Malaysia in Kuala Lumpur.
Besides teaching Professor Wardi is involved
in research on low-cost building techniques for mass rural applications.
The drawings and photographs of the four regional houses
are taken from unpublished studies by Jabatan Senibina,
carried out between 1976 and 1980. The work has been printed with permission
from the University Technologi Malaysia and is their copyright.
All other photographs are by Parid Wardi Sudin.

The population of Malaysia is not one homogeneous group but made up of Malays from various islands of the Malay Archipelago. This diversity of population is the consequence of a continuing regional movement of people, dating back to the time of the Malacca Sultanate in the 15th century. The rise and fall of regional powers, the coming of European colonialists, the ever present inter-island trade and Malaysia's favourable position on the ancient trade route to China, have contributed to the constant movement of people, from the region and beyond, into the Peninsular. In the process, various groups, including non Malays have settled in the country and helped to introduce a variety of regional domestic architecture. Although it has been suggested that the Malays of the region share common cultural roots, each group however has developed independently, producing its own cultural and architectural identity and form.

Over time, the confrontation of the various immigrant cultures, among themselves and with the local cultures, has served to dull the sharp distinction between the various regional and local architectures. The process, and extent to which these changes have taken place, is difficult to trace for lack of continuity of evidence. Since the most common building material used is timber, examples of early houses no longer exist. Even the major surviving examples which are less than 100 years old are difficult to study because they have either been modified, vandalised or are in a serious state of disrepair.

The process of cultural interaction has not produced a single architectural style. While a common cultural base can be identified, strong regional, cultural and architectural form and character persists.

Thus there exist today, a variety of Malay domestic architectures, traceable to their distant origin in the various islands of the Archipelago, but different in many ways from their original styles. It is possible to identify several types of domestic architecture such as the *Kedah* house, the *Banjarese* house, the *Bugis* house, the *Minangkabau* house, the *Kelantan* or Thai house, the *Perak* and *Pahang* house, etc. (Research by the Universiti Technologi Malaysia on traditional architecture through the process of measured drawings have produced yet more variations of house form than is commonly known. Classification of the various house types is yet to be undertaken.) The distribution and location of the various house types usually relate to the original area in which the people settle and the names are usually referred to by either the name of the people or the State in which they are most commonly found. The *Minangkabau* house refers to the people and they are found almost exclusively in Negeri Sembilan. However the *Kelantan* house which refers to the State in which the houses are found, is not exclusive to Kelantan but can be found in Trengganu and Thailand.

The house, beyond satisfying basic family and community needs and the expression of man's aspiration, is a cultural process. It embodies man's search for a deeper meaning of human existence, his relationship with the environment, his fellow beings and his Creator, *Allah*.

The basic community unit, kampong (village) is not an expression

of geographical locality, but of human relationship determined by such factors as kinship, common livelihood and mosque congregation. Often the physical size of a *kampong* is determined by the hearing distance of the mosque *gendang* (drum), which traditionally summons people for prayer. The kampong, guided by a council of elders, represents an integrated social unit bonded by kinship and the sharing of common facilities, problems and hopes. Community participation extends beyond participation in the rites of passage. It includes mutual economic aid and house construction. Often the boundary between individual, family and community responsibility is difficult to identify.

Thus the design and construction of the house is determined by the dictates of society and customs, rather than individualistic wishes. Although the houses in any given kampong seem to vary in form they do not constitute a departure from social and cultural norms but represent the various stages of growth. Variations of family income and wealth means that initially the family can only afford a house of a certain size. As the family accumulates its wealth, the house is extended. The process continues until a 'standard' house is completed. This also means that houses for those with position and wealth are bigger and more elaborate. In some areas, the

process is entrenched as a custom, thus reinforcing the relationship between status and house style.

Conceptually the house extends beyond the physical structure to include the whole of the immediate environment. Often the concept of house and village is freely interchanged. The expression *'Pulang ke Kampong'* which means 'to return to the village', is often used instead of returning home to denote the oneness of the concept of house and village.

Although in recent times the location of a house is determined by legal land ownership, the house site and its orientation is still carefully selected in order that they are in the hilly rather than wet location, that the house faces the morning sun and orientated towards the *Qiblat* in Mecca.

The process of house construction depends on the owner's wealth. Rich families engage the *tukang,* (master craftsman) while poor families build through the process of community self help — *gotong royong.* However through the institution of the site selection ceremony, house erection ceremony and house warming ceremony the whole community is involved, irrespective of who builds.

Although each regional house type has its own distinctive character, they all share several common features. Without exception, they are all on stilts and have pitched roofs. They are all open plan, regulated by construction modules and have several levels. They use similar building materials and the construction system allows for the additions and the recycling of components.

The logic of building on stilts has more to do with health, comfort, aesthetics and understanding the building material rather than the oversimplistic reason to avoid

Top: Malacca house: note traditional thatched roof and new roof of sheet metal.
Left: Malacca house, gable end view. The decorative carvings provide ventilation to the loteng *(attic).*

Malacca House

flood. The people, through their architecture, crafts, games, pastimes and boat-building activities have shown a wealth of creative potential.

In some settlements annual flooding does occur, but the numbers are few. If floods are the strong reason for building on stilts, it is strange to see the Chinese, who for a long time have lived side by side with the Malays subjected to the same floods, continue to build their houses on the ground.

The pitch roof is logical in hot wet climatic conditions. The steep pitch, permits rapid removal of rain water and creates a high sloping ceiling ideal for inducing air movement, ventilation and the escape of hot air — hence comfort.

Two elements which typify the Malay house is the open layout and the use of levels. Often the house has only one room, apart from the separation between the *rumah ibu* (main house) and the *rumah dapor* (kitchen section). While spaces are assigned specific functions and status by their location and levels, these are not totally fixed, but are dependent on the occasion. So while women are assigned to the *rumah dapor* (kitchen section), they are not forbidden in the main house. However during religious and social functions such designations are observed and the women congregate in the *rumah dapor* and the men in the *rumah ibu*. The function of spaces therefore changes with activities. The eating space may at night be converted for sleeping by the introduction of sleeping mat, pillow and mosquito net. Thus the layout of the house responds to a continually changing use of space.

The common building materials used are timber for the structure, floor and walls, and *nipah*, *rumbia* (sago) or *bertam* thatch for the roofs. Till today the preferred wood is *chengal*, but this is costly and difficult to get. So alternatives such as *merbau* are used. In poorer families round timber is often used for posts and beams and split areca nut trunk used for flooring. In areas such as Perlis where *bertam* and *bamboo* are plentiful the walls are woven from these materials. *Rumbia* and *nipah* leaves folded into two around split bamboo or spilt areca nut trunks, form the basic roofing materials; and at times walling material of houses adjacent to low lying areas. Near coastal waters *nipah* is extensively used, further in-land it is *rumbia*. *Bertam* is a hill plant and can be woven into roof thatch by itself.

While the material evidence collected from current studies on the Malay domestic architecture points to a rich cultural heritage and inter-relatedness of Architecture to the cultural process is yet to be fully understood. Many theories and speculations exists but the hypothesis is yet to be tested. Meanwhile the knowledge, as only the *tukangs* know, is being rapidly lost.

The house, located at Permatang Serai Road, Merlimau, Melaka, was built by Penghulu Mohd. Natar's father Haji Abdul Ghani bin Abdul Majid in 1894 at a cost of $33,000 ringgit (approx. US$15,000). Four *tukang* (master builders) were responsible for the construction. Manaf Bopeng from Merlimau was the carpenter for the house structure, Mahmud Kelantan from Kelantan executed all the decorated wood carving, Sahal bin Junit painted all the decorations and carvings and Pendek Pendekar acted as general carpenter. In 1925 when the house was modified by Penghulu Abdul Ghani, the same *tukang* were asked to do the work.

The design is based on old Malacca traditional houses and shows considerable Chinese influence. Traditionally, Malacca houses reflect the owners status. Ordinary the Malacca house contains a short *anjung*, and a *rumah induk* (main house) with one or two rooms, a *loteng* (attic) and a *rumah dapor* (kitchen) at the rear. For the middle group, the house consists of two houses, *rumah induk* and *rumah belakang*, which extends to the rear, and an *anjung* which contains a *serambi*. Houses for *Demang* (Regional Heads), *Penghulu* (local head) and *Tok Sidang*

(village head) usually have two or three houses, extending to the rear, *rumah dapor*, a long *anjung* and a large *serambi* to accommodate a large gathering. A feature common to all Malacca houses and Minangkabau houses of Negeri Sembilan is the inclusion of an attic within the roof space. Both sides of the roof gable are closed by *timba layar*. The houses usually follow a proportion of ½:1:1 between the raised portion on stilts, the main body of the house, and the roof respectively. The act of only slightly raising the house on stilts, apart from the obvious practical advantages of avoiding water penetration and damage to the timber, makes the house aesthetically much more pleasing. Malacca architecture generally reveals a considerable Chinese influence, from as early as the 14th century. In the case of Penghulu Mohd. Natar's house, the extent of this influence is more than usual on account of his business partnership with a Chinese businessman, Pua Beng, who commission several Chinese workers to modify the main staircase and the gateway to the *jemuran*. Further, two of the original *tukangs*, Mahmud Kelantan and Manaf Bopeng, learned their craft from a Chinese carpenter. Consequently the main staircase was decorated with richly coloured glazed tiles often found in Chinese architecture. The roof to the gateway used Chinese tiles and has a *sulur bayung* at the end of the roof ridge. The colours of the interiors, decorative fences and wood carvings were also bold and vivid, of red and gold.

Above: A typical Malacca house seen from the front showing a spacious halaman *(lawn), elaborate* tangga *(stairs) and* anjung *(reception area). The entrance stairs in concrete replace the traditional timber steps. This is a recent development which has been influenced by Chinese architecture both in terms of form and colour.*

Left: A typical Malacca house in Jasin Road, Malacca.

Right: The main curved-form staircase is richly decorated with ceramic tiles.
Below: The main entrance to the right of the photograph shows the elaborate staircase. This part of the house which forms an informal reception area — the serambi — *is completely open. The central section shows the main house area — the* rumah induk — *and in the rear the kitchen and dining buildings separated by a courtyard. The full height windows of the main house are louvred and often kept open during the evenings.*
Note: Plan below is of the original house, the present staircase has been changed.

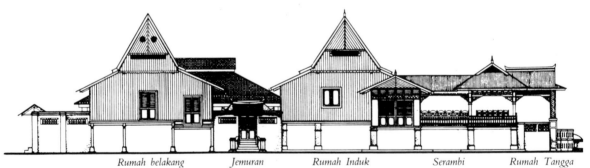

| Rumah belakang | Jemuran | Rumah Induk | Serambi | Rumah Tangga |

Side elevation

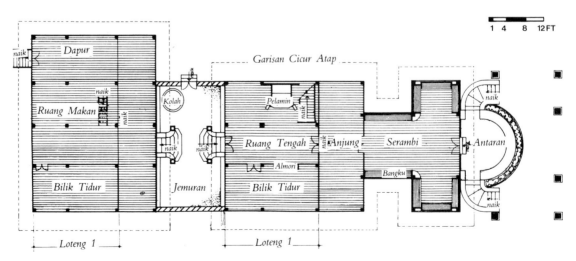

Plan (Before 1925)

Kelantan House

While most major architectural examples are often associated with aristocracy, the Malay house of Pulau Panjang, belonging to Tuan Haji Nik Salleh, is a commoner's house, built by ordinary people. It is also one of the oldest example of traditional architecture in Malaysia. The owner, a man of great pioneering spirit and exceptional ability, commissioned two local *tukang*, from Pulau Panjang to build the house for himself and his family. The original house consists of seven units, of three building types. A *rumah tiang dua belas* (twelve pillared) consisting of *rumah ibu, rumah tepi sungai* and *ruang lahar,* a *rumah bujang* consisting of *rumah dapor* and two *rumah bujang,* and a *rumah perabung lima* consists of *rumah selasar.*

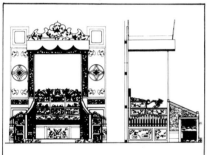

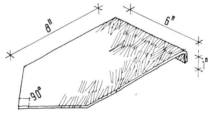

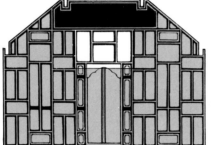

Top: Typical details of wood carving above the doorways.
Left: Roof tile found exclusively in Kelantan and Trengganu. The tile originates in Thailand.
Left, below: Typical system of Kelantan house wall panel.
Below: Detail of relief panel and khat *painted in Air Perada Emas (gold colour) on a red background.*

During a wedding the bride and groom would sit at the pelamin *and be blessed by members of the family. The* pelamin *shows remarkable Chinese influence in its decorative motifs and colours.*
Top: The pelamin *with the* tiang seri *in the foreground.*
Above: The tiang seri *is a ceremonial pillar and is the most important column in the house.*

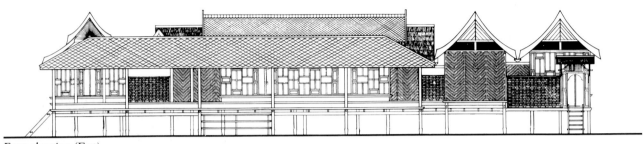

Front elevation (East)

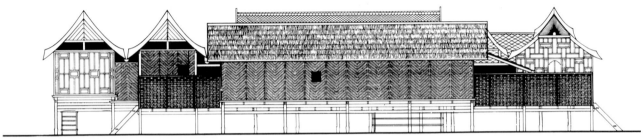

Rear elevation

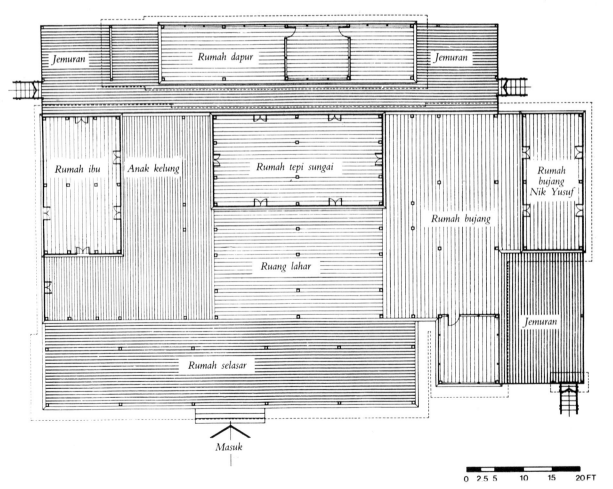

Plan

Jemuran

Rumah dapur

Jemuran

Rumah ibu

Anak kelung

Rumah tepi sungai

Rumah bujang Nik Yusuf

Ruang lahar

Rumah bujang

Jemuran

Rumah selasar

Masuk

0 2.5 5   10   15   20 FT

Minangkabau House

The Minangkabau house which originates from Sumatra is found mainly in Negeri Sembilan. Two of the best known examples are the *Istana Ampang Tinggi* and *Model Rumah Melayu,* both in Seremban, Negeri Sembilan. The house has a basic rectangular form and supports a curved roof. The ridge is lowest in the middle and slopes upwards at the ends. The gable end, which projects well beyond the gable end wall, slopes inwards. Unlike the Kedah house the Minangkabau house have no *rumah tangga.* Entry is direct into the main house.

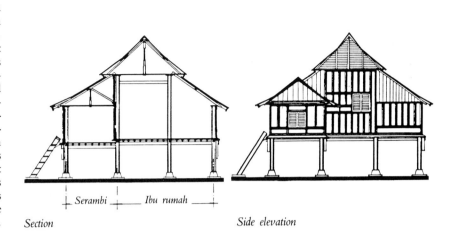

Section

Side elevation

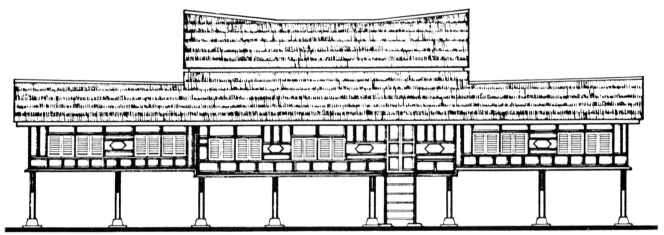

Front elevation

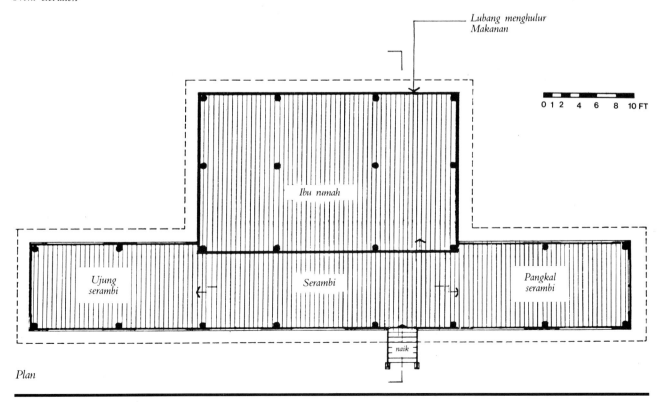

Plan

Perak House

One variation of the *Perak* house, found mainly in the Northern States of Kedah, Perlis, Penang and north Perak, is characterised by their use of the *bumbong lima* roof and the *anjung* which projects at the front of the house. The *anjung* is a formal guest area and reflects the wealth of the family. Poor families may not have an *anjung* to their houses. Richer families may have two *anjung* called *anjung dua beradek* or three *anjung* called *anjung tiga beradek*.

The house consists of three main structure, *rumah dapor* (kitchen), *rumah ibu* (main house) and *anjung*, often constructed in that order too. Poor families would initially construct the *rumah dapor* to serve all family needs. As the family's circumstances improved, the *rumah ibu*, and sometimes the *anjung* is added. Otherwise the *anjung* is added as a third stage, this being of better material, constructional standard, and finish. An intermediate structure, located midway between the *anjung* level and ground level, is the *rumah tangga*. This is usually only partially enclosed and serves at the main entrance and place for informal discussion.

Top, right: Perak house at Kuala Kangsar. The house is typical of the houses where the anjung *protrudes predominantly from the* rumah ibu *(main house) and the* rumah tangga *at the side. The* jendela *(long vertical window) provides excellent ventilation. The traditional roof tile has been replaced with iron sheeting.*

Opposite, bottom: A more recent but less typical Perak house. While retaining the basic Perak house form it does not have a rumah tangga. *The ground floor enclosures are not typical and the windows do not reach the floor, due to economic reasons, but meets a woven matting curtain wall.*

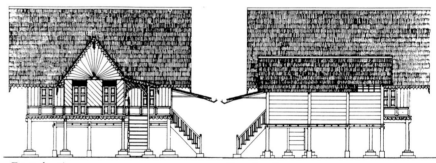

Front elevation   *Rear elevation*

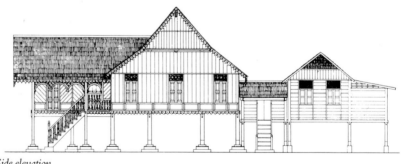

0 1 3 6FT

Side elevation

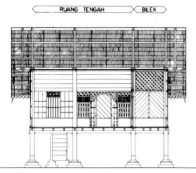

RUANG TENGAH	BILEK

Section BB

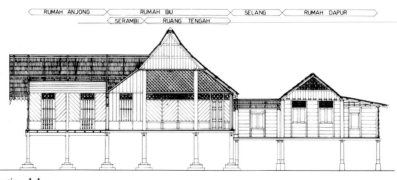

RUMAH ANJONG	RUMAH IBU	SELANG	RUMAH DAPUR
SERAMBI	RUANG TENGAH		

Section AA

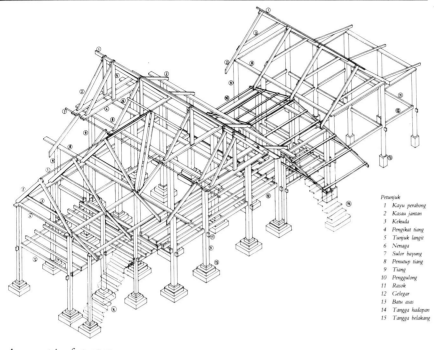

Axonometric of structure

Petunjuk
1 Kayu perabong
2 Kasau jantan
3 Kekuda
4 Pengikat tiang
5 Tunjuk langit
6 Nenaga
7 Sulor bayung
8 Penutup tiang
9 Tiang
10 Penggulong
11 Rasok
12 Gelegar
13 Batu asas
14 Tangga hadapan
15 Tangga belakang

RUMAH ANJONG RUMAH IBU SELANG RUMAH DAPUR

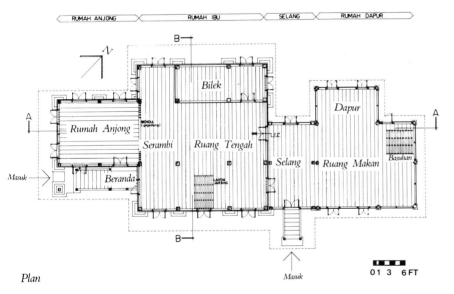

Plan

Masuk

01 3 6 FT

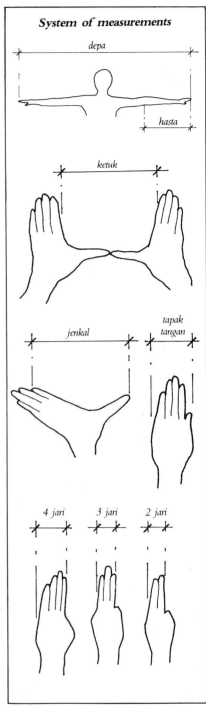

System of measurements

depa

hasta

ketuk

jenkal   tapak tangan

4 jari   3 jari   2 jari

Glossary

Anjung/serambi: Formal/informal reception areas.
Beranda: Verandah
Bilek tidur: Bedroom
Halaman: Lawn
Jemuran: Open area between kitchen and main building
Jendela: Window
Loteng: Attic
Pelamin: Bridal dais
Ruang makan: Dining room
Ruang tengah: Centre room
Rumah dapur: Kitchen
Rumah ibu/rumah induk: Main house

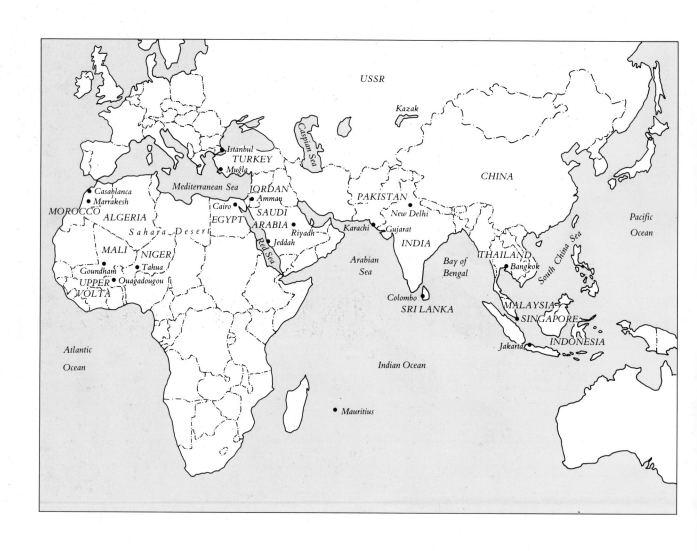